ALSO BY CHRIS WOODING:

MALICE

CHRIS WOODING

ILLUSTRATED BY DAN CHERNETT

■SCHOLASTIC

First published in 2009 by Scholastic Children's Books
An imprint of Scholastic Ltd
Euston House, 24 Eversholt Street
London, NW1 1DB, UK
Registered office: Westfield Road, Southam, Warwickshire, CV47 0RA
SCHOLASTIC and associated logos are trademarks and/or
registered trademarks of Scholastic Inc.

Text copyright © Chris Wooding, 2009
Illustration copyright © Dan Chernett, 2009
The right of Chris Wooding and Dan Chernett to be
identified as the author and illustrator
of this work has been asserted by them.

ISBN 978 1407 10394 5

Typeset by M Rules
3D Cover produced and printed by Magnetic Advertising
Book printed by CPI Bookmarque Ltd, Croydon, Surrey

Papers used by Scholastic Children's Books are
made from wood grown in sustainable forests.

1 3 5 7 9 10 8 6 4 2

www.scholastic.co.uk/zone

MIDLANDS

Sixes and Lights

1

"I have to show you something."

The trees outside the window hissed and rustled in the warm August night. Leaves and twigs skittered across the paved yard, chasing the wind. A three-quarter moon glowed bright through gaps in the blanket of cloud that hung over the Midlands.

Heather was standing at the window of Luke's bedroom, looking down. In the yard, a black tomcat sat perfectly still, looking back at her.

She turned away from the window. It was a typical boy's room, just like her brother's. Plain, cream-white walls, a few dog-eared posters of bands she didn't care about, crumpled clothes strewn over various surfaces. Luke was digging through a drawer, searching for whatever it was he wanted to show her. She watched him while his back was turned. Skinny, red-haired, popular at school. Everyone liked him, but he'd been her friend first. They'd played together since they were five.

3

Downstairs, all was quiet. His mum was out tonight. They had the house to themselves, so he'd invited her over. He had a secret, and Heather loved secrets.

He shut the drawer and sprang on to the bed, freckled face alive with excitement. He had something hidden in his arms.

"Come here," he said, patting the bed. She scrunched up to him excitedly, crowding in to see what it was.

Then he showed her what he'd taken from the drawer, the secret he wanted to share, and she felt herself go cold.

She took it from him and stared at it. It was a flat rectangle of black wax paper. On the front was an elaborate emblem in red. Six points, arranged in two V-shapes, one on top of the other. The points were joined to form an M, and surrounded by a hexagon.

It was still sealed, but she knew what was inside. She'd heard about Malice.

"Where did you get it?" she asked him.

He nudged her with his shoulder. "Don't worry about that. Open it."

She glanced at him uncertainly, then at the comic in her hand. She was suddenly aware of how the silence had deepened in the house. Like the building was holding its breath. Even the wind outside had died.

She handed it back to him, a little too quickly. "You open it."

Luke gave her a strange look and shrugged. "Okay. *I'll* open it."

He carefully unsealed the wax paper sleeve and slid out the comic. Heather looked away.

"What's wrong?"

She didn't reply. How could she tell him, without sounding stupid? She had no words for the creeping unease that was making its way up her spine.

"You want to read it together?" he asked.

She nodded. There was nothing else she could do. She didn't want to admit that she was afraid; not to him, anyway. There wasn't anything to be scared of, no matter what the rumours said. After all, it was just panels and pictures, ink and paper.

The first tale was about a girl caught in a labyrinth of glass and wire. She was trying to find her way into the centre, where there was some kind of prize waiting for her, but the wire kept twisting around and trying to entangle her, and the walls shifted continually. A mannequin made of sharp bits of metal was limping after her through the maze, leaving a trail of oil behind it. It was catching up to her fast.

Luke looked at Heather to check she'd finished the page, then turned over to the next. She did her best to keep reading, but each panel was worse than the last. The horror mounted until she couldn't bear it any more. It was the girl's eyes that scared her the most. There was real fear in those eyes. She was running for her life.

Heather looked away. "I don't like it," she said quietly.

"Why not?"

She couldn't explain. She knew she was being ridiculous, but she didn't care. "I don't want to read any more."

Luke shut the comic and put it aside, a grin of amazement spreading across his face. "You believe it, don't you? You actually believe those stories!"

She got up and stalked to the window. Arms crossed, she stared furiously down into the yard. She hated being made fun of. He was such a boy. Couldn't he see she didn't want to read some dumb comic!

The black tomcat was still sitting in the same spot, staring up at her.

"Hey, come on!" said Luke, springing off the bed. She turned around to face him, but she wouldn't meet his eyes. "Look, I'm sorry. I didn't mean to scare you."

"I wasn't scared," she murmured, but she was going bright red and she knew it. She always blushed when she lied.

"Those kids in the comic, they're not real kids," Luke said. "It's just a rumour. They say the artist looks in the Missing Persons sections of the papers and he uses those kids as models for the characters in the story." He made a face. "It's pretty sick, I suppose."

"Can't they arrest someone for that?" Heather asked.

"Probably, if they could find him," Luke replied. He scratched the back of his neck awkwardly; then his eyes lit up. "I'll prove it to you!"

"Prove what?" she asked, but he was already hurrying over to the wardrobe. He took out a small plastic carrier bag and a stone bowl, then sat down cross-legged on the floor. He put the bowl down and waved at her to sit opposite.

She did so. Something was sinking in her stomach. She should put a stop to this now. She should just walk out and leave him to it.

You're being a child, she told herself. *Malice, Tall Jake . . . it's all just a story.*

She made herself sit still and tried to keep the discomfort off her face as Luke shook out the contents of the plastic bag. She even managed a weak smile when he looked up at her, eagerly, as if seeking her approval.

One by one, he put the ingredients into the bowl. Preparing the ritual. They both knew how to do it. A lot of kids knew how to do it, even if few of them ever dared.

First, a black feather. Second, a twig. Third, a knot of cat fur.

"I got the first two from the woods," he said. "The third, well, I've got an aunt with cats. Ten minutes in her living room and you'll have an inch-thick layer of fur settle on you. You can only take fur that's been shed or that's come off naturally. That's the rules."

The fourth ingredient was the tear. He offered no explanation for that one, but he brought out an old plastic camera-film case and tipped it over the bowl. A single drop fell out and soaked into the cat fur.

Next he brought out the nail scissors, tipped his head to one side and cut off a small piece of his hair. He scattered it into the bowl, and held out the scissors to her. She shook her head quickly. A fleeting disappointment showed in his eyes, but he didn't push the matter.

"And the sixth ingredient," he said, holding up a cigarette lighter. "Fire."

"You think it's a smart idea to light a fire in your bedroom?" she asked, hoping he might reconsider. But he just gave her a look. *Stop being a wimp.*

He held the flame to the small cluster of ingredients in the bowl. The cat fluff ignited, becoming a small burning wad in which sat the twig, the feather and Luke's red hair. Heather turned her head away and coughed at the reek.

"Tall Jake, take me away!" he said. He glanced over at Heather with a sly grin. "Tall Jake, take me away! Tall Jake, take me away!"

"Stop it," Heather murmured.

"Tall Jake, take me away! Tall Jake, take me away!"

"*Stop it!*" she yelled.

"You have to say it six times, Heather, before the fire burns out."

"Don't."

"It's not real! I'm just trying to prove it to you!" He was getting annoyed now.

"I don't want to know! And I don't want to hear

anything else about that comic!"

He stared at her. Then he said, very deliberately: "Tall Jake, take me away."

Heather sucked in her breath. Something terrible was going to happen; she just *knew* it. A fierce gust of wind rattled the window and sent the trees into a frenzy. She surged to her feet and looked out, as if she could catch sight of whatever was coming. The cat had disappeared from the yard.

The seconds scraped by. Heather was tensed, waiting, waiting.

But everything remained as it was. The terrible thing didn't happen.

"See?" Luke said. He stood up. The tiny blaze in the bowl had gone out. "I just wanted to show you. There's nothing to be scared of."

Heather let her breath out slowly. She couldn't help a nervous giggle of relief. He giggled with her, and she realized that he was relieved too.

"You believed it!" she said. "After everything you said, you believed it!"

He grinned. "Well, maybe. A bit. Pretty exciting, though, huh?"

She swatted him across the chest. "I nearly died, you idiot!" she laughed.

But then . . .

. . . the lights went out.

10

2

Moonlight seeped through the window, painting everything in ghostly blue and white. The warmth had drained from the room. The bed, the wardrobe, the crumpled clothes were drenched in shadow.

Luke shoved his hands into his pockets. "Well," he said. "I think we can call that bad timing." But the joke came out weak. If this sudden darkness was a coincidence, it was a little *too* coincidental.

"I told you! I told you not to do it!"

"Hey," he said. "It's just a fuse." He stood there a moment; then, realizing what was expected of a boy in a situation like this, he reluctantly added: "I'll go down to the cellar and trip the switch."

Heather shook her head frantically. "He gets you when you're alone."

"What?"

"Tall Jake. He comes when you're alone. That's what they say."

He gave her a steady stare. "It's just a fuse," he said again. Because he didn't dare think what else it might be.

She went quiet.

Luke went to the door of the bedroom, put his hand on the doorknob, hesitated.

Don't go out there. Stay here where it's safe.

No. He couldn't chicken out in front of Heather. It had

been a long time since he'd been afraid of the dark.

But it wasn't the dark he was afraid of. It was the sense that he'd done something awful, and now he couldn't take it back.

"I'll just be a minute," he said.

His bedroom door opened out on to a landing with a banister that overlooked the lounge. He pulled the door shut. The silence smothered him. Through a skylight in the ceiling, he could see the clouds racing across the face of the moon.

It's just a power surge. You'll go trip the switch in the fusebox and everything will be okay.

Slowly, carefully, he walked along the landing towards the stairs, his hand trailing on the banister. The air tasted strange. Tinny and sour. Maybe there was a storm on the way.

Down in the lounge, something muttered.

He froze. Listened hard to the silence. A gust of wind whistled across the roof and shook the skylight.

Nothing. Imagination.

He crept to the top of the stairs, looking down into the lounge. The furniture sat quietly in the sharp moonlight. Beyond, at the edges of the room, there was only empty, aching darkness. He would have to cross that room to get to the kitchen and the cellar door. Suddenly, it seemed a long way.

Just get it over with, he told himself. He steeled himself and then hurried down the stairs before he could change his mind.

There was a faint skittering noise from the landing, the sound of tiny clicking claws, like rats. He looked up in alarm, in time to see something small dart across the gap at the top of the stairs. His heart jumped painfully in his chest.

What was that?

It had been too quick for him to be certain he'd seen anything. It could have been a trick of the moon-shadow. But the sound . . . he was *sure* he'd heard a sound.

He thought of Heather, still up there in his room. He thought of how it would look if he just turned around and went back right now.

No. He wasn't going back. He might be scared, but he wasn't going back.

He stepped out into the lounge and walked boldly across it. Once he'd started, he had to keep going. His nerves crackled: he knew that something was going to pounce on him at any moment. He went past the TV, past the sofa, towards the doorway that led into the kitchen. The attack could come from anywhere. . .

But it didn't. He reached the doorway, safe and well.

The kitchen was long and thin, with a counter running along the right side. A door at the end stood open, leading to a utility room where they kept the washing machine. Luke felt his confidence grow a little. There was no place to hide here, no corners where something might lurk.

He heard the slow creak of a door opening elsewhere in the house.

There was no mistake this time. He'd heard *that* for sure. He was breathing heavily now, trembling a little. The metallic taste in his mouth was stronger. It felt as if there was electricity in the air.

Then he realized: Heather! Of course, it was only Heather, who'd got bored or frightened and had wandered out of his room.

But it sounded like it came from downstairs...

The lights. He needed to get the lights on. He couldn't bear the dark any more.

He hurried through the kitchen and into the utility room. It was cluttered with junk: boxes of screws, bits of tubing, Dad's old tools that he left behind when he went off to live with Diane. The washing machine, half-full, sat beside the door to the cellar. The key was in the lock. The fusebox was just inside the door. He could reach in; he wouldn't even need to go down the stairs into the blackness.

Then he saw the torch. Dad's torch, sitting on his tool shelf. He snatched it up, turned it on. Light! Cold electric light pushed back the heavy dark. He shone it around to be sure that nothing was in the room with him, then reached for the door to the cellar.

There was a long, crooning mewl from the other side.

Luke's blood turned to ice. He stopped, his hand on the key.

There was something in the cellar. It began to scratch at the door. Claws on wood, scraping, scraping.

Luke stepped back in horror, shaking his head. "I didn't

mean it," he whispered. "I didn't want you to take me away. It was just a game."

Something thumped on the upstairs landing. The scratching stopped, and there was another piteous mewl from behind the door.

Suddenly Luke realized what that sound was, and he began to laugh nervously. If he hadn't been so scared he would have identified it straight away.

It was a cat. There was a cat trapped in the cellar. He reached for the key and turned it.

The long mewl stretched, deepened, and became a horrible, rasping cackle.

Luke cried out and leaped back from the door as it began to swing open. His torch illuminated the gap in the door for the briefest instant, and through it he saw a dreadful hint of something that was all horn and bone and fang.

A blast of light dazzled him, and Luke screamed. The door swung open . . .

. . . but there was nothing there.

He stared at the doorway to the cellar. No monster waited for him, only steps leading down into the musty dark. The lights had come on throughout the house, dispelling the terror, and a key was rattling in the front door. It opened with a noisy clatter, and then there was the familiar bustle of his mum returning from her night out.

"Luke! I'm home!"

Life on a Cliff

1

"Don't let go! Don't you let go!"

Letting go was the last thing on Seth's mind, but his fingers were burning, his hands were claws of pain, and he couldn't hold on much longer. A bead of cold sweat was trickling down his spine, beneath his thin T-shirt. He looked down at the rocks fifteen feet below him and tried not to think how it would feel when he landed on them.

Nononodon'tletmefall!

Kady was at the top of the cliff, her face a picture of horror framed between loose blonde pigtails. Beneath her, the rock sloped gently down a short way, ending suddenly in a sheer drop. Seth was hanging there, arms splayed, toes scrabbling for a hold, grip weakening with every moment that passed.

"I'm throwing you a rope! Just don't let go!" Kady yelled at him, then disappeared from view. He was too heavy for her to pull up; she was searching for somewhere to affix the cam, a spring-loaded device that gripped cracks in the rock to provide a secure anchor for the rope.

Kady was a keen climber, and her dad had supplied her with all the equipment she needed. She'd come laden with ropes, carabiners, cams, harness, climbing shoes, belay gloves, and a half-dozen other little devices that Seth didn't have a name for. The first chance they had, they'd ditched her parents and gone hunting for something to use them on.

Except Seth *didn't* use them. He'd insisted on free-climbing the cliff without any safety gear at all. It hadn't really seemed all that high.

The strength was ebbing from his arms and back. He struggled blindly for purchase with his feet, scraping at the stone with his trainers. His palms were stinging and raw from dragging down the slope when he fell. He wanted to adjust his grip, but he didn't dare.

I can't hold on, he thought. *I can't hold on.*

"There's nowhere to fix it!" he heard Kady shout from above, her long California vowels floating away over the sunny Derbyshire hills. She was starting to panic. "Seth? Seth?" She appeared again, looking down at him. "There isn't anywhere to fix it!"

"Well, don't tell *me*!" he cried, voice high with desperation. "Find somewhere!"

She dithered for a few more seconds before disappearing again. He could hear her scrabbling around, searching for a suitable place to wedge the cam.

Wait ... what was that he felt? He pressed down with his toe. A lump of stone, just enough to provide grip. He adjusted his foot. A solid hold.

His arms were trembling uncontrollably. His fingers were going numb. One thing was certain: whatever help Kady could give him, it would come too late.

He gritted his teeth. One chance. One try. He hoped he had the strength for it.

He bent his knee and launched off from the foothold, propelling himself up and forward. Throwing his arms out, he reached for a fold in the rock further up the slope – and somehow, his fingertips caught and held it. He pulled with the last of his energy. One knee came up enough to get over the cliff edge, and with a last lunge he flung himself flat against the slope.

He lay there, his cheek against the warm rock, while his heart slowed and the circulation came back to his fingers. After a few moments, he began to laugh with sheer relief. He wasn't going to fall. His hands burned and everything ached, but he felt great.

A short while later, he heard the thump and slither of a rope next to him.

"Just in time," he said, voice dripping with sarcasm.

"What did I say when we started this climb?" Kady called. "Always use your safety gear!"

"Then where would be the fun?" he replied.

Kady started to laugh with him as he grabbed on to the rope. "Get up here, you idiot!"

2

They lay on their backs on the great slab of stone and watched the clouds glide sleepily through the burning blue sky. All around them, the folds of the Peak District dipped and rose, its solemn green ridges broken by outcroppings of ancient rock like the one they'd just conquered. England was being hammered by an early August heatwave, a surprise window of perfect weather in an otherwise typical British summer. School was still far enough away to be an empty threat, and the days were theirs for the taking.

"Don't you wish it could always be like that?" Seth asked.

"Like what?"

"Like you're about to fall off a cliff."

Kady made a quizzical noise.

"I'm serious," he said. "I mean, want to end up like your parents? Going to work, coming home, watching TV till you go to bed? Where's the fun in that?"

"That's *your* parents, not mine," she replied.

Seth didn't say anything else. After a moment, Kady raised herself on her elbows and looked at him strangely. He was staring up at nothing, face grim. Loose black hair hung untidily over his forehead and ears. His fringe blew restlessly in the faint breeze.

"Does it really bother you?" she asked. He shrugged,

which was as good as a yes. She nudged him with her foot. "There's no law says you have to turn into your parents. Don't worry about it, huh?"

She lay back down, pillowing her head with her hands, soaking up the heat. It was a different kind of sun here than back in California. Her childhood had been spent running on beaches, splashing in the Pacific. Every day was glorious, the skies were clear, and even in winter it was never truly cold. In England, the sun was rare, more precious because there was never enough of it, and the winters were long and dreary.

At times like this, if she shut her eyes, she could almost imagine she was home.

"What's up with Luke?" she asked, to change the subject.

"He went down to London to see his dad on the weekend," Seth said. "Maybe it didn't go so well."

"He's been weird all day. Wandering off on his own and stuff. It's not like him."

"I'll talk to him."

"Hey, about what just happened: don't mention it to my parents, alright? I don't need another safety lecture."

"Parents," Seth murmured. "When are they gonna realize that we know what we're doing?"

"Seth, not ten minutes ago you almost fell off a cliff."

Seth grinned. "The key word is *almost*."

3

They met Kady's parents back at the car park of the tourist centre, where a small shop sold maps to ramblers and several cafés dealt with hungry visitors.

"Hey, they're here!" cried Kady's mum, Alana, as she saw them approaching. "Did you have fun? Oh my God, Seth, you're hurt! What happened to your hands?"

"I fell over," Seth replied. "Nothing serious."

"Nothing serious? Well, it looks serious to me, mister! Let me get you some cream for that, I know I've got some somewhere."

"No, really, it's alright. I just scraped them a bit."

"I can't hear you!" she yelled, because she was already rummaging around in the boot of the car, where there was a cooler packed full of health drinks, a box of home-made carb-free salads, and a range of herbal ointments.

Kady rolled her eyes. "Just go with it," she said. Seth knew better than to resist. Alana always carried an arsenal of natural remedies for any ailment, and never missed a chance to deploy one. Seth had learned not to sneeze near her if he didn't want to be force-fed strange-tasting teas for the rest of the day.

Kady's stepdad, Greg, was British, a former software engineer who had invented a program for calculating traffic density in cities. Though it sounded enormously dull to Seth, it had made him rich enough to retire at forty. He wasn't Kady's biological father, but she called him Dad – her real dad wasn't worthy of the name. Greg was a quiet, simple man who just wanted an easy life, and he walked around with a slightly bewildered air, as if he couldn't quite work out how he'd ended up married to a manic ex-hippie from the States. Maybe it was something to do with her being a professional hypnotist. Seth entertained himself now and then with visions of Kady's mother mesmerizing her wealthy husband with a swinging pocket-watch.

Greg was eating soy ice cream out of a Tupperware carton and gazing wistfully at a nearby burger van. Alana had put him on a no-meat diet six months ago, and ever since then he'd been sneaking bacon sandwiches whenever she wasn't around. Seth had never known a more reluctant vegetarian.

Alana was smearing Seth's hands with foul-smelling paste when Luke arrived. "The wanderer returns!" she said. "Been off communing with nature?"

"Just had some things to think about, Mrs Blake." He glanced at Seth, then looked away.

"How mysterious!" she said. She finished up with Seth and then wiped her hands on a cloth. "Well, if we're all here, I suppose it's time to go home."

4

Kady had the uncanny ability to fall asleep within ten minutes of entering any moving vehicle, so Seth wasn't

22

surprised to find her head on his shoulder on the journey back. Alana was chattering away to her husband in the front seat, who wasn't really listening. The radio was playing Joni Mitchell, and Luke was looking out of the window at the countryside.

Seth was worried. Kady had been right: the way Luke had acted today wasn't like the Luke he knew.

They'd met on the first day of secondary school and had been friends ever since. Luke's dad used to run archery classes down at the leisure centre, and they'd gone together every week for a year until Seth got sick of shooting at static targets. Over time, they'd had shared various obsessions: BMXs, trading cards, comics, football. They'd fought and made up, walked every inch of their little village domain, and talked about everything worth talking about. Between them, they'd made life in Hathern just about bearable.

In all that time, he'd never known Luke to clam up like this. Even when Luke's parents suddenly divorced, he'd always been able to discuss things with Seth. Something must have really shaken him.

"Hey," he said quietly, over Kady's head. Luke turned away from the window and looked at him. "You okay?"

Luke cast a quick glance at Kady's parents, then at Kady herself. For a moment he hesitated; then he leaned closer and said quietly:

"You ever heard of Malice?"

Kady stirred uneasily in her sleep and muttered something, too softly to hear.

"What about it?" Seth asked.

Luke lowered his voice still further, until it was hard to hear over the music and the sound of the engine. "I found a copy."

"You read it? What's it like?"

His face clouded. "It's strange. It's pretty strange."

"Luke, what's up? Something's been bothering you all day."

"I just had to think, that's all. I didn't know if I should tell you. Like, I didn't want to involve you."

"Involve me in *what*?"

Luke motioned to Seth to keep his voice down. In the front seat, Kady's mum talked on, oblivious.

"Last night, I said the chant. You know the one."

"Tall Jake, take me aw—"

Seth was shushed before he got any further, and he was surprised to see fear on his friend's face, just for an instant.

"What?" he protested. "It's just a daft legend. You burn a few things, say the chant six times, then Tall Jake comes to take you away. There's a million stories like that. I've heard ringtones that were scarier."

Luke shook his head. "Listen, I'm not kidding. I said it and some really weird stuff happened."

Seth had to resist the urge to scoff. Surely Luke was having him on?

"What kinds of things?"

Luke opened his mouth to speak, but then Kady stirred

24

again, distressed by something in her dream, and burrowed further into Seth's shoulder.

"Are you alright back there?" said Alana, looking through the gap between the seats. "Aah, look at my little baby! Isn't she sweet?"

"We're fine, Mrs Blake," said Luke.

"Let me know if you want any organic oatcakes."

"Will do," said Seth, but not before he'd noticed the fleeting grimace on Greg's face. The only way Greg wanted oatcakes was if they came wrapped in ham.

Alana returned to the task of educating her husband about trans-fats in doughnuts, and Seth tried to resume his conversation with Luke.

"What kinds of things?" he said again, but the moment had passed. Luke didn't want to talk about it now. Instead, he whispered:

"I'll call you tomorrow. You can come over, I'll show you the comic. I'll tell you the whole thing then."

Seth nodded. "Alright. Tomorrow."

"And keep it a secret from you-know-who," he said, thumbing at Kady. "I don't want anyone else involved in this if I can help it."

Seth frowned. "Are you sure you're okay?"

But he'd gone back to looking out of the window, and he didn't answer.

Lost Connections

1

When Luke hadn't phoned by seven in the evening, Seth decided to call his mobile. But the voice on the other end of the line belonged to Luke's mother.

"Hello, Seth. If you're looking for Luke, I don't know where he is. He must have been up and out early this morning. Left his mobile behind, too."

"Oh. So you don't know when he'll be back, then?"

"Your guess is as good as mine," she said. "I'm sure he'll turn up later."

"Could you ask him to call me as soon as he gets in?"

"I'll do that."

"Even if it's late, it doesn't matter."

There was a pause on the other end. Luke's mother had detected something amiss. The slight tinge of concern in his voice.

"I'll tell him," she said, but he could hear her suspicion.

Seth hung up the phone and slumped against the headboard of his bed. Outside his window, the sun was low and sullen, throwing long shadows across the rooftops of the neighbouring houses. The little village of Hathern was always quiet, but today it disturbed him. He'd had a bad feeling ever since his conversation with Luke in the car.

He snorted at himself in disgust. He was letting himself get spooked by the stories. He wouldn't be surprised if Luke was winding him up on purpose, just for a laugh.

So he's gone out early and he forgot I was supposed to be coming round. So what?

But he would *never* have left his mobile.

Seth got up and paced the room. The corners and cupboards were crowded with the debris of previous hobbies: his archery bow, a basketball, BMX parts, a paintball gun, a white *gi* suit from his brief kung fu phase. In the end, he got bored of all of them. He wasn't allowed to try the more extreme sports like skydiving yet, but he didn't think even they would satisfy him. The danger felt fake. Somehow it didn't seem right if you were all strapped up in safety gear. It didn't seem right that you had to pay money to do anything exciting, to book a time to face peril. It made it all seem a bit ridiculous.

His dreams were full of new frontiers, of explorers like David Livingstone, the first European to cross the African continent, or Neil Armstrong, the first human being ever to set foot on the Moon. Kady had fascinated him with tales of Lewis and Clark, the men who trekked across North America long before anyone had mapped it, and of Columbus and Magellan, the great sea voyagers. These were men who cast themselves into the unknown, far from help, facing terrible and extraordinary danger. These were his heroes.

Today's explorers were sponsored by soft drink corporations, all their challenges pointless because there was nothing left to explore. Seth couldn't care less if someone went around the world in a balloon. They had satellite navigation, engineers to monitor their progress, rescuers waiting to pick them up if they failed. He considered it cheating.

And what about the heroes? Where were they? There *were* no heroes now, only stars: sports stars, film stars, rock stars. All pampered and rich, advertising products they probably never used.

Downstairs, he could hear his parents settling down to dinner in front of the TV. Some quiz show or another, a lot of laughing and clapping. He couldn't talk to them about Luke. His parents were the last people he'd go to with a problem.

It wasn't that he didn't love them, although he would only admit it grudgingly. It was just that they were incapable of understanding him. It was as if, one day, he'd woken up speaking a different language. They just didn't get it.

He stared at his phone, willing it to ring. It didn't.

2

<Kadybug> sup cuz?
<Jezzibel828> no much. U?

28

<Kadybug> same

<Jezzibel828> how things in england?

<Kadybug> meh. miss home

<Jezzibel828> LOL that is your home

<Kadybug> u know what I mean. wish I cud come back and c u in SF again

<Jezzibel828> san fran disco is de nuts, tis true

<Kadybug> remember when we were in berkeley and luce was doing that thing with the squishie and it went all over you?

<Jezzibel828> ROFLMAO yeah I was totally mad

<Jezzibel828> u know how hard goth stuff is to wash?

<Jezzibel828> all that lace and leather ☺

<Kadybug> price of joining the dark side

<Jezzibel828> *makes mental note to extract dry cleaning money from luce's still-warm corpse*

<Kadybug> no wait it totally wasn't in berkeley

<Jezzibel828> where was it then?

<Kadybug> don't u remember?

<Jezzibel828> thought it was in berkeley

<Kadybug> whatever it was funny

<Jezzibel828> yeah

<Jezzibel828> so things are ok?

<Kadybug> sometimes I get real mad at mom for making me come here

<Kadybug> like, she just decided dad was the one for her and she upped sticks and went chasing after him

<Kadybug> took me with her

\<Kadybug\> greg dad, not dad dad
\<Jezzibel828\> that's so something my mom would do
\<Jezzibel828\> spose they are sisters . . . ☺
\<Kadybug\> didn't care that I wanted to stay
\<Jezzibel828\> u like your dad tho, right?
\<Kadybug\> course I do. I'm happy she's happy. Just wish they could be happy back home.
\<Kadybug\> wait I remember
\<Kadybug\> we were in golden gate
\<Kadybug\> not berkeley
\<Jezzibel828\> that's right
\<Jezzibel828\> I remember now
\<Jezzibel828\> LOL not even close
\<Kadybug\> afhsjdd;;l'\
\<Kadybug\> sorry
\<Jezzibel828\> ????
\<Kadybug\> cat walked over my keyboard
\<Kadybug\> wait phones ringing. seth. brb.
\<Jezzibel828\> oooOOOOooooOOooOoh!!!
\<Jezzibel828\> <3 <3 <3
\<Kadybug\> shutup

3

Kady swivelled in her chair and picked up her mobile just before it switched to answerphone. Marlowe made a lunge, but Kady was too quick, and snatched it away from him before he could pounce on it.

"Nice try," she told the silver tabby. He began to groom himself resentfully next to her keyboard. "Seth. What's up?"

"Not a great deal. Luke was meant to call me. You seen him today?"

"I haven't. Mom had me helping out at a bake sale for blind mongooses or something."

"Do mongooses go blind? Wait, is it mongooses or mongeese?"

"Mongii?"

"What was it *really* for?"

"They want to fix a church roof. Doesn't matter to Mom, as long as it's a good cause."

"Anyway, so Luke's nowhere to be found. His mum hasn't seen him all day and he's left his mobile."

"That's weird. Normally you can't peel that thing out of his hand."

"Exactly."

Kady scratched Marlowe under the chin. "Did you ever talk to him about what was up yesterday?"

A pause. "That was what today was about."

Kady got the sense that he was being evasive, but she couldn't be bothered to chase him on it. At that moment she was wrapped up in a sleeping bag like a caterpillar, wearing a towelling robe and drinking a mug of Fairtrade organic sugar-free calorie-free hot chocolate that Alana had delivered her. Her plans for the night involved a long bath, reading a bit and then aimlessly trawling the Net. She was too relaxed to get worked up about anything.

"You're stressing, aren't you?"

"I've just got this bad feeling, Kady."

"Seth, he's fine. He's probably just gonna stay at a friend's place. Or he's hiding a secret girlfriend from us," she added jokingly.

"He's been talking about Leia a lot, now I think about it."

"There you go. Wait, Leia from chemistry? Really? Her?"

"I never told you."

"My lips are sealed," she said, already composing a message to her cousin Jess in San Francisco, typing with her free hand. Since technically she was using her fingers and not her lips, she figured it was okay. "Listen: it's cute that you're worried about him, but you're not his keeper. You always think you're responsible for everyone."

"Well, you've got to look out for people, don't you? What kind of world is it otherwise?"

Kady took the mobile away from her ear and stared at it in disbelief. Seth would occasionally come out with things like that. She could never decide whether she found it sweet or just naïve.

"He's down, that's all," she said, returning the phone to her ear. "Don't panic. He'll tell us when he's ready."

"Yeah, you're right."

They said their goodbyes and hung up. Kady played with Marlowe while she waited for Jess to reply to her gossip, but Jess was away from her computer and wasn't answering.

"I guess things aren't so bad here, are they, cat?" she asked Marlowe, whose eyes narrowed with pleasure as she ruffled his fur and scratched his chest. "I've got Seth and Luke and everyone. And I'd never have met you if I hadn't come here. Could be worse, right? Right."

But she couldn't pin down this feeling of restlessness she had. It had been with her ever since she came back from San Francisco.

They'd been living in London, having moved in to Greg's place after the marriage. Kady had been happy enough, as far as she could remember. But then she'd gone to stay with her aunt and cousin in San Francisco for four months. She forgot why; probably she just wanted to get out of the newlyweds' way for a while. Those four months seemed like a pleasant blur now.

But this creeping unease had begun when she returned to London. Soon after, they moved to Hathern, a tiny village in the Midlands. Alana didn't like big cities, and as usual, her decisions were made for everyone. Greg didn't complain; he never did. And Kady wasn't given a choice.

So she ended up here, itchy and unsettled, with the same feeling of being out of place that had bothered her for almost a year now.

Her gaze drifted over to the ornament that sat on her bookshelf. It was one of only two souvenirs she'd brought back from her trip, bought on a whim in an antique shop near

Haight-Ashbury. She must have thought it was interesting. It certainly wasn't pretty, but there was something weirdly attractive about it. It was a squidlike monstrosity, like an ancient kraken of the deep, its grey stone tentacles wrapped around a cloudy egg of some whitish mineral. The egg was semi-transparent, and if you stared deeply into it, it reflected the light in strange ways.

She opened a drawer of her desk and drew out the other souvenir: a white play-money dollar bill. At least, that was what she thought it was. It was made of a papery material and embroidered around the edges with spiked designs. The number 1 was printed on both sides, within a thorny circle. Jess had found it on a day out, lying on the sidewalk, and after they'd puzzled over it for a while, she'd given it to Kady. "For luck," she said.

Marlowe mewled inquiringly, wondering what could possibly be more important than him. Kady laughed and nuzzled him. He was one of the best things about coming here. Several days after they'd arrived in Hathern, while they were still moving in, he'd turned up at the door. She'd let him in, given him some food, and he'd simply stayed. He looked well-fed and healthy, and he didn't seem like a stray, so Alana insisted that they put up notices in case anyone had lost a cat. When nobody answered after two months, they gave in and kept him. Alana thought that anything so unusual had to be fate.

When Marlowe had absorbed enough attention to be temporarily satisfied, he slipped off the desk and went to sleep on the bed. Kady put the white dollar back in the drawer. She flicked off the computer screen and went to take her bath.

Marlowe, only pretending to sleep, watched her go through slitted eyes.

Drawing Blanks

1

The police asked a lot of questions, but nobody had any answers. A slow, terrible fortnight passed. A fortnight full of speculation and rumours, of worry and fear and anger. And still Luke didn't come home.

"How could he do that to his mother?" Seth's dad demanded to know, as he sat half-watching a rerun of a comedy show from the seventies. "That poor woman's raising him on her own and this is how he thanks her."

"Mike! Shush! That's his best friend," said Mum, motioning towards where Seth was slumped on the couch, flicking through a magazine with a scowl on his face.

But Dad couldn't possibly admit that he'd been insensitive – that would be like admitting he was wrong – so he blundered on. "I don't care who he is, there's no excuse for that kind of selfishness. Linda's a wreck. And who do you think pays for the police that—"

"Jesus, Dad!" Seth snapped, throwing the magazine down in his lap. "He's not *run* away, he's been *taken* away!"

TallJaketakemeaway

His parents stared at him, shocked. Dad, with his weary-looking face, a balding dome of a head. Lumpy cheeks from childhood acne and a long, thin nose. Small eyes that never seemed interested in anything. Then there was Mum: small, plump, with greying blonde hair cut in a short, efficient, masculine style. Jolly, silly, always ready with a smile – but it was the smile of somebody who didn't understand what she was smiling at.

They didn't even seem like people to Seth. It was as if there were two worlds for adults, divided by an invisible barrier: the world of the Living and the world of the Dead. The Living dressed up and looked good and they went out and did things like go to the theatre and eat in restaurants. They laughed and sparkled. The Dead drifted back from their jobs every day and sat in front of the TV, and every day they got a bit podgier and duller, and they only bought cheap, functional clothes because there was no point looking good when you never went out.

Seth looked at his parents, and he was afraid. He was afraid that he was a child of the Dead, and nothing he could do would stop him turning into one of them.

"Don't you dare talk to me like that!" Dad said, as surprise curdled into anger.

"Mike, he's just upset, don't—"

"I won't be spoken to that way in my own home, Jane!"

Seth brushed the magazine off his lap, and walked out of the room. He couldn't stand it. He was sick with worry for his best friend and his dad had managed to make it something to get angry about. As he pulled open the front door, he heard Mum calming Dad down, urging him not to follow.

"Leave it, hmm? He doesn't mean it. You'll just make it worse."

Seth almost walked into Heather, who was standing on his doorstep. He jumped a mile, hand going to his heart. Heather shied away with a little scream. They looked at each other and Seth gave a quick and breathless laugh.

"I think I just died," he said.

But Heather wasn't up to even the weakest of jokes. She just stood there looking at him, hovering on the edge of tears. He didn't know why, but he had the impression that she'd been waiting outside his door for a long time, and hadn't rung the doorbell.

"Hey, are you okay?" he asked. But she just bit her lip and shook her head. "Want to come in?" Another shake.

"I need to tell you something," she said. "About Luke."

Seth looked over his shoulder at the door to the living room. Then he stepped out into the warm night and closed the front door behind him.

"Come on," he said. "Let's walk."

2

Luke's mum had been crying. Her eyes were red, and she was wiping her nose with a handkerchief when she opened the door. Seth saw the faint hope die on her face at the sight of him and Kady standing there. Perhaps she'd believed, just for an instant, that it would be Luke.

"He hasn't come back," she said, her voice flat.

"We know," Seth said. He'd been nervous enough about facing her; the sight of her in this state made things worse. Her blonde hair was tangled and she seemed to have aged ten years. Coming face-to-face with her grief made him awkward. If he'd believed for one moment that Luke had really run away, it might have made him furious at his friend's selfishness. But he didn't think that was even a possibility now. Not since his talk with Heather.

"What do you want?" she asked. She drew out a cigarette and lit it.

"Can we have a look around Luke's room?"

She blew a jet of smoke and waited for an explanation.

"It's just . . . maybe there's something there. Something that you or the police didn't find. Like, something that only his friends would recognize."

She stared at him for a long time, until he began to fidget. He glanced at Kady, who was just as bewildered at her dangerous silence.

"Is that okay?" he asked, when he could bear it no longer.

"You knew something was wrong, didn't you?" Luke's mum said slowly. "When you called that day."

Seth felt himself reddening. But how could he answer? How could he tell her about Malice?

"I just . . . I had a bad feeling," he said lamely.

She grabbed him by the shoulder, looked him in the

eyes. He could smell the smoke and tears on her. "If you know anything. Please. . ."

Seth felt something twist in his gut. He wanted to spill everything, no matter how ridiculous. She was so desperate to have her son back.

"I don't know where he is," he said, and that, at least, was the truth. "I want to help if I can."

She held on to him for a few moments, squeezing his shoulder hard. Then she let go, and walked back into the house, dismissing them. She'd left the door open. Kady shrugged and shooed him inside.

They walked into the living room, closing the door behind them. Luke's mum had gone to sit in an armchair, watching TV. She ignored them totally now. They went past her and up the stairs, giving her a wide berth, as if she were a wounded animal, liable to snap at them at any moment.

At the top of the stairs was the landing, overlooking the lounge. Seth stopped there. The door to Luke's room was at the end.

"What's up?" Kady asked.

Seth was remembering Heather's frightened whisper, the things she'd said. You couldn't fake that kind of fear.

"*There was something on the landing. After the lights went out.*"

"*You sure it wasn't just—*"

"*I'm sure, Seth. It wasn't pipes, and it wasn't floorboards. It wasn't anything like that. It sounded like . . . I don't know . . .*

like rats. No, like a hundred little crabs, all running around. Clicking their claws."

But there were no signs on the landing that anything had been there.

Kady hustled past him impatiently. She didn't understand what the delay was. He hadn't told her anything about what Luke or Heather had said. He didn't want to try and explain it to her when he wasn't sure what he believed himself. He didn't want to contaminate her with the fear, the superstition, the legend of Malice.

They went into the bedroom. There was a wardrobe with a mirror set into one of the doors, a desk, a chest of drawers, posters of footballers and bands. An unremarkable room. So why did it feel as if a weight had settled on his shoulders when he stepped across the threshold? Like a cold, damp blanket?

"It smells like gas in here or something," Kady said, wrinkling her nose.

"Yeah," said Seth absently. He walked over to the wardrobe and looked into the mirror.

TallJaketakemeaway

He reached out to open the wardrobe.

"*But it was the . . . it was the thing in the wardrobe that. . ."*

"*Wait, there was something in the wardrobe?"*

"*In the dark. The door just came open. It just . . . it just came open and I couldn't see inside."*

"*Heather, wardrobe doors come open all the time, it's—*"

"*There was s-s-something b-b-breathing in there!"*

Heather had got hysterical at that point. It had taken Seth ten minutes to calm her down. Whatever she'd seen or heard, it had scared her witless.

He opened the door with his fingertips. Inside, only clothes.

There was a beep as the computer booted up. Kady had settled herself in the seat in front of the screen.

"I thought we were looking for something to help us find Luke?" he said.

"We are. You nose around, I'll check his computer." When Seth gave her an odd look, she added: "I know you can barely use email, Seth, but most of us keep our lives on our PCs nowadays. If there's anything, it's in here." She began to clatter away at the keyboard.

Seth went over to the chest of drawers against the far wall. Amid the clutter of action figures, comics, and music magazines were little pieces of Luke's life: a medal he'd won for archery; a quartz rock he'd found on holiday; a photo of him and his dad in front of some cathedral somewhere, his dad's arm around his shoulder.

An unbearably awful sensation swept over Seth as he stared at them. For the first time he began to think that he might never see his friend again. That whatever had happened, had happened for ever.

No. He wouldn't let that be true. He'd find his friend. He'd make this right, somehow.

He pulled open the drawers. This was where Luke kept it, Heather had said. This was where he hid the comic. The drawers were the first thing Seth would have checked, anyway. Luke's favourite hiding place. Catapults, firecrackers, secret plans for mayhem: they'd all been stashed in this chest of drawers at one time or another.

The top drawer was full of socks and boxer shorts. He dug through them, found nothing. The next one held crumpled T-shirts, stuffed wherever they would fit. He burrowed in, and his fingers brushed against something cold. He pulled it out.

Malice.

It was in his hands. A black wax-paper cover, stamped with a spiky red M inside a hexagon. The top edge had been carefully pulled apart, and the comic lay inside.

Suddenly, he didn't want to look. He didn't want to find out. He glanced at Kady, who was bringing up menus on Luke's PC, a pencil between her teeth, thoroughly engrossed. Her back was to him.

You have to. Do it for Luke.

He reached inside, grasped the comic, slowly began to pull it free of its cover.

"Hey. Look at this," said Kady, taking the pencil from her mouth.

Seth let the comic fall back and let out a breath. "What is it?"

"Come here."

He left the comic on the bed and went over to the computer, where a street map was being displayed. "Check it. I went through his History and he'd run a search for this location."

Seth stared at the screen. It was a maze of streets, with

a little arrow pointing to one of them. "You did what?" he asked, bemused.

"You really don't know *anything* about computers, do you?" Kady grinned.

Seth shrugged. He couldn't see the point of them. They were such a waste of time. Most of his friends spent hours every night on the Net, often chatting online with the very people they'd just seen at school. Why they couldn't just meet up in person, or use the phone, was a mystery Seth had never been able to get his head around. He was just too much of an outdoor person to spent his whole life in his bedroom.

Kady tapped his skull with the end of the pencil. "Okay. Layman's terms. Your computer saves a record of every website you look at. So I went through the records. He was looking up this address in London."

"In London? Do you know when?"

"Sure. He did the search on . . . August third."

Seth made some mental calculations. "That was a few days before he went down to London to see his dad."

"Easy enough to make a little side trip."

"So what's there?"

"According to this, nothing special. It's just an address."

She looked at Seth. Seth looked back at her.

"You want to go, don't you?" she said.

"You could tell your dad we were going shopping for the day. He wouldn't mind you going to London. He lets you do anything."

"Of course he wouldn't mind; I used to live there, remember?" She raised an eyebrow. "I guess you expect him to pay for you as well?"

"Kady, he's got more money than God. He'll spring for two tickets if you ask him."

Kady sighed. "It's a long way to go for—"

"Please," said Seth, grabbing her arm. "This is really, really important to me."

She searched him with her gaze, puzzled by the desperation in his voice. "Sure, Seth," she said, her voice gentle. "If it means that much to you. We can go tomorrow."

He let her go and sat down on the edge of the bed. "I have to show you something."

She scooted over on the office chair. "What'd you find?"

He held up the black comic. "You ever heard of Malice?"

A strange expression settled on to Kady's face. Slowly, she reached out and took it from him. She put it in her lap and stared at the emblem.

"Kady?" Seth prompted. "You okay?"

She shook her head as if to clear it. "Sorry . . . I guess I just spaced out there for a. . ." She trailed off. "I think I've heard of it. I mean, I must have heard the name."

She reached inside and pulled out the comic, then flicked through the pages with her thumb.

"What's the deal?" she asked him. "Is it meant to be a joke or something?"

Seth took the comic from her and opened it. He turned

to another page, then another. This couldn't be right. This wasn't what Heather had said Malice was like.

He went through the comic cover to cover,

BUT

EVERY

SINGLE

PANEL

WAS

BLANK.

London

1

The atmosphere was strained on the journey from Loughborough to St Pancras.

It was a few miles' walk over fields and down lanes to get from their little village to the nearest train station, so Kady's dad ran them into town, with only a small detour to pick up a bacon sandwich on the way. Kady kept her father's secret. It was their little shared rebellion against Alana. Kady didn't actually like meat all that much herself, but she ate it because she knew her mother disapproved.

They caught the train and settled in for the hour-and-a-half journey south. Instead of chatting as she usually did, Kady plugged her iPod into her ears and looked out of the window. Seth couldn't help feeling rejected.

Things hadn't been quite right between them since they'd argued the night before.

"It's beyond stupid, Seth. You're telling me you think he's been taken by a character in a comic book?"

"*I'm saying it's something to do with the comic. I don't know exactly what.*"

"*Seth, face it. He's run away. That's all there is to it. I don't care what Heather said and I don't care what he told you about 'weird things happening'. He's run off. End of.*"

It wasn't like her. Usually she would have played along, even if she was only humouring him. She was always up for a bit of an adventure. She could find fun in the most mundane things. He supposed she was more worried about Luke than she let on.

She'd agreed to go anyway, since it meant so much to him, but she was making no secret that she was only doing it because he needed her to. He couldn't afford a ticket on his own, and he'd never ask his parents. He could imagine the conversation that would ensue.

"*Going shopping? In London? What do you want to do that for? You can just go to Leicester. There's everything you need in Leicester.*"

And God forbid he actually told them the real reason he wanted to go. They'd have him in therapy faster than he could blink.

Am I just being ridiculous? he thought as he sat on the train, listening to the tinny drumbeat coming from Kady's headphones. But he didn't feel that he was. Sure, he knew how it sounded. But he'd seen the look on Luke's face, and he'd heard the fear in Heather's voice, and he'd sensed something when he walked into Luke's room. Maybe he didn't have any answers yet, but he just *knew* something was going on. Something bad.

They arrived in St Pancras and caught the tube to New Cross. By that time, Seth's penance-by-iPod was over. Kady's bad mood had worn off and she was chatty again. She rabbited away about anything that came into her head, although Seth noticed she avoided the subject of Luke and the comic entirely. Just being in London energized her. She loved the buzz of the busy city.

But Seth saw something different as they stood on the hot and crowded tube. He saw a huge grey warren full of tired-eyed commuters. Everyone had an iPod or a book, shutting out the other passengers. Nobody looked at or talked to anyone else. Hathern was tiny and boring, but everyone knew everyone. London was vast and anonymous, and nobody knew anyone.

They came out of the tube into a dirty maze of broken-down streets, one of the many grim suburbs of London that the tourists never got to see. It was the kind of English day where you couldn't even see the underside of the clouds. The sky was just a dull, miserable haze, weakening the sun until you could barely tell where it was.

"Well," said Kady, surveying their surroundings. "Shopping opportunities slim to zero, I'd say."

"Come on," he said. "Sooner we find this address, sooner you get to tell me this was a waste of time."

"I already know it's a waste of time," she said brightly. "Don't think I won't be calling in some big favours for this."

Kady had printed out a map from Luke's computer, but they still got lost and had to backtrack several times. There was an annoying lack of street signs, and the rows of terraces all looked the same.

"Well, whoever lives at this address, they sure don't want to be found," Kady commented after their third wrong turn.

Finally they came across the road they needed, which ran alongside a low railway bridge. On one side there were only crumbly garden walls. On the other there were several small garages and repair shops nestling beneath the train tracks. The whine of saws and drills came from within. Mechanics with grimy faces joked with one another as they lay beneath cars.

"A garage?" Seth said, disappointed. He'd hoped for better answers than this.

"Number 42," Kady said. "Come on. We're nearly there."

They walked down the road a little way, past the garages. There were some empty and abandoned shops, their windows soaped over. A dry cleaner's, a minicab firm . . .

. . . a comic shop.

Seth's heart leaped as he saw it. There it was, at number 42. A small shop buried far from the shopping districts, hidden beneath a railway bridge. It had tiny, dark windows and there was graffiti on the brickwork. Its sign – which was the only thing that looked new about it – bore the words Black Dice Comics.

2

For some reason, Seth expected a bell to tinkle when he pushed open the door. It had the kind of musty, stale atmosphere of an antiques store. Instead there was only an expectant hush.

The shop was chilly and uninviting. Dirty windows killed the light as it struggled in. Three rows of shelves were on their right, full of comics arranged in careful order. On their left was a counter, and at the end of it was an open door.

"Hello?" Seth called.

The shopkeeper appeared through the door at the end of the counter, pulling it closed behind him. He was a mountain of a man, well over six feet tall, with broad shoulders and a large gut. His head was entirely bald, there was no stubble on his face and, disconcertingly, he had no eyebrows at all. He was wearing a waistcoat over a white shirt, and braces to hold up his grey trousers. Rubbery lips spread in a smile as he saw them, but the smile didn't reach his eyes.

"Welcome to Black Dice Comics," he said, and Seth was surprised to hear a high, breathy voice coming from this massive figure. Girlish, with a faint lisp. He mopped his forehead with a handkerchief. "Feel free to look around."

"Thanks," Seth mumbled. He was unnerved by the man's lack of eyebrows. Between that and the greasy sheen of his skin, it made him seem like a half-finished waxwork.

He and Kady wandered into the shop, heading down

one of the aisles. Seth scanned the shelves, looking for issues of Malice. Somehow, he knew it wouldn't be that easy.

"Okay, I'll admit it," said Kady quietly. "This is a little weird. I mean, there being a comic shop here."

"This has to be where he got it from," Seth said. "He heard about it from someone, he looked it up, and when he came down to London to stay with his dad, he paid this place a visit."

"I'm still not buying into this," Kady warned. "Just saying it's weird."

But Seth was excited. This was the place. He just knew it. He took down an issue of *X-Men* and flicked through, so as not to look suspicious.

"What's up with the shopkeeper's face?" he muttered, glancing down the aisle. The shopkeeper was pretending not to watch them.

"Alopecia," Kady said absently. "It's when you don't have any hair on your body at all. Even eyebrows and eyelashes." She caught his look. "Hey, my mom buys every health magazine they publish. You just pick up stuff."

Seth put the comic back. "Right. Let's do this."

"Do what?"

But Seth was already walking up to the counter, where the enormous man stood. The shopkeeper fixed the smile back on his face. Seth couldn't shake the feeling that those tiny black eyes were regarding him like a shark about to devour a smaller fish.

"Are you looking for anything special?" the shopkeeper breathed. "We have a very wide selection."

Seth leaned close. The shopkeeper leaned in to listen. He smelt of sour sweat. "I'm looking for the new issue of Malice," Seth said.

The shopkeeper stared at him, calculating. The smile never left his face, but Seth felt the temperature drop a degree or two.

"Surely you know that Malice is only a rumour. A silly schoolyard tale."

"Or maybe it's just too dangerous to sell along with the other comics," Seth suggested.

He had the sense that he was being judged. There was no doubt in his mind that the shopkeeper knew what he was talking about; the question was whether he would admit it or not. If Malice was everything the rumours said it was, someone who sold it would have to be very careful who they trusted.

The shopkeeper studied him for a long time, and he never dropped that horrible fake smile of his. Seth stared back at him, refusing to break his gaze. There was something repulsive about this man, about his smell and his voice and his appearance – but if he could help them find Luke, Seth wouldn't look away.

Eventually the shopkeeper straightened. "I'm sorry," he said. "You must be very disappointed. But I'm afraid Malice doesn't exist." He dabbed at his forehead with his handkerchief again.

"I've seen it," Seth told him.

"Really?" The shopkeeper looked sceptical. "I find that very hard to believe."

"I've *seen* it," he said again, more firmly this time.

The shopkeeper just looked at him, that cold smile on his fishy, rubber-lipped face. "Lucky you."

Kady swore loudly from the back of the shop, and there was the sound of dozens of comics falling in a paper avalanche.

"Oh, you confounded little wench!" the shopkeeper cried, hurrying out from behind the counter. "What have you done?" He passed by Seth without another glance and huffed his way over to where Kady was kneeling, picking up the comics she'd knocked over. "No, you'll put them back all wrong!"

Seth didn't think twice. He went around the side of the counter and into the back room, through the door the shopkeeper had emerged from.

The room was small, with no other exits, and was lit by a single bulb hanging from a wire. It was full of boxes and stacks of bound comics. Seth could still hear the shopkeeper fussing distantly, but the shelves blocked his view.

His heart was racing. He didn't want to be caught back here. He wasn't the kind of boy who was afraid of getting into trouble – ordinarily, the idea of getting shouted at by some fat guy was no big deal – but the shopkeeper was a different matter. Seth had looked into his eyes, and he'd seen emptiness. No passion, no pity. The dead eyes of a predator. That man could be very, very dangerous if he chose to be.

Quickly, he began searching through the boxes. He pulled one open, looked inside. A horror comic, something about zombies. He shifted a few small stacks of manga and dug into the box beneath, but it was all superhero stuff. He glanced back at the doorway, but he was too far inside the room to see much of the shop outside.

Boxes and boxes, and he was running out of time.

Come on, Kady. Keep him busy. Just a few minutes more.

<h1 style="text-align:center">3</h1>

It wasn't easy to create the appearance of clearing up while at the same time creating more mess, but Kady was learning fast. She floundered about amid the pile of comics, acting flustered, shoving comics clumsily back on the shelves so that she knocked other ones off.

"You ham-fisted troll! Can't you do anything right?" the shopkeeper howled. He was kneeling next to her, snatching things out of her hand. "Just leave them alone! Leave them!"

"No, it's my fault," she protested, gathering up another handful of comics and jamming them roughly on to the shelf. "I mean, I couldn't let you—"

"You don't put *Green Lantern* with *Spider-Man*!" he cried. "And that one isn't even supposed to be in this section! Just stop, you awful scab!"

"I feel terrible," Kady said, yanking a handful of graphic novels from his sweaty grip. "At least let me do these."

"Get off!" he said, grabbing them back and tearing one of them. "Now look what you've done!"

"I think *you* did that."

Kady was getting anxious. There was still no sign of Seth

and she didn't know how much longer she could stall the shopkeeper with this farce. It had been a spur-of-the-moment thing to help Seth out, to pull down a bunch of comics and give him some time to snoop. What had made her do it? She realized it was the shopkeeper himself. She could tell, even from where she'd been standing, that he'd been lying to Seth. That meant there *was* a comic called Malice. And maybe, just maybe, Seth was on to something.

While the shopkeeper was scrabbling around in the pile of comics, she glanced over his shoulder towards the front of the shop. Where was Seth?

The shopkeeper looked up, and she shifted her gaze back a fraction of a second too late. Those small, dark eyes went from hot to freezing cold in an instant. He turned towards the counter.

"Where's your friend?" he asked slowly.

Kady tried to think of something cocky, something to divert his attention, but she came up blank. She could only shrug. The enormous man got to his feet, scowling.

"Now where could he have gone?" he muttered to himself. Kady heard something menacing in that creepy, high-pitched voice.

The shopkeeper began striding towards the counter. Kady got up and hurried after him. "Hey, listen, I'm looking for some early *Sandman* issues, you think you could show me where they are?"

But he wasn't listening. He strode onward unstoppably, out from between the shelves, and now they could see that there was no sign of Seth anywhere in the shop. There was only one place he could be.

The shopkeeper's eyes narrowed, and he went hurrying towards the door to the back room, which was hanging slightly ajar.

"Are you listening to me?" Kady cried, tugging at his arm. "You know *Sandman*, right?" Her attempts at delaying him seemed feebly transparent now. He shook her off irritably and threw open the door.

Kady held her breath. The man's bulk blocked the doorway. She couldn't see inside.

After what seemed like a long time, the shopkeeper turned around. No smile on his face now.

"It seems your friend has run out on you," he said.

Kady gave a little laugh, mostly from relief. "Oh yeah, he's always doing things like—"

"I do hope none of my stock is missing, young lady," he breathed. "Or I shall be a very angry person."

Kady swallowed. "I'm just gonna go, huh?" she said, backing away. "I guess you're not in the mood for customer service."

She turned and made for the exit, half-expecting to feel a meaty hand clamp down on her shoulder. But she got through the door and out to the street, and he didn't try to stop her.

It had begun to drizzle. She walked fast, hands in her pockets and her head down, trying to put some distance between herself and the shopkeeper in case he changed his mind. Something about that man frightened her. She only started to relax when she was quite a way down the road.

Seth appeared from the doorway of one of the garages and fell into step next to her.

"You got what you wanted?" she asked.

"Yeah."

"Let's see it, then."

"Not yet," he said. "Not till we're in a safe place."

"*What?*"

Seth's voice was grim, allowing no argument. "Not till we're in a safe place."

4

Seth was punished by iPod on the journey back, as he had been on the way there. This time Kady was furious that he wouldn't show her the comic. She told him he was being paranoid, but Seth refused to give in. Things were adding up for him now: Luke's disappearance, Heather's story, the comic, the man in the shop. There would be an answer at the end of this trail; he was sure of it.

I didn't want to involve you, Luke had said. But they *were* involved.

They were picked up at the station by Kady's dad and taken back to her huge house on the edge of the village. Kady had bought a few things from Carnaby Street, to add weight to their story about going to London for a shopping trip. It would have seemed odd if they had come back empty-handed. Her mother demanded to see all her purchases before they were allowed to go upstairs. Kady listened to Alana's delighted cries with barely disguised impatience.

As soon as they decently could, they escaped to Kady's room and shut the door behind them.

"*Now* show it to me!" Kady snapped.

Seth pulled the comic out from where he had it hidden inside his coat. It was still in its black wax-paper sheath, the dark red M on the front. Kady took it from him. She had the same strange expression on her face as when he'd shown her the copy in Luke's room.

"I found dozens of them in a box in the back," he said. "I slipped behind the counter and out just before the shopkeeper came to look."

"This one better not be blank," she said, and without ceremony she tore it open and pulled out the comic within.

It wasn't. Seth saw that straight away. The cover showed a boy's face, half in shadow and screaming, the title MALICE scratched across the top as if by the tip of a claw.

Kady couldn't wait any longer. She opened the comic to the first page, and almost immediately Seth saw her go white.

"What? What is it?"

She flicked through several more pages. "Oh, no, no," she murmured.

"What?" Seth demanded, getting scared now.

She looked up at him, puzzlement and horror on her face. "The boy in this comic . . . it's *Luke*."

The Thing in the Wardrobe

1

Kady woke with a scream.

She almost fell out of her bed before she realized that nobody was chasing her. She sat up in the darkness, clutching at her duvet, heart thumping against her breastbone. Safe in her bedroom. Fleeting visions from her nightmare came back to her. Visions of some hunched thing wearing a cowl and a cloak, with round lenses for eyes that glowed a cool blue. It had been carrying a flamethrower, shooting burning jets after her as she fled through the corridors of some strange temple. She could still smell her charred hair.

The door burst open and she screamed again. Her mother screamed back.

"Honey, it's just me!" said Alana, turning on the light. She hurried over, knelt down by the bed and began frantically smoothing Kady's hair back from her brow. "Are you okay? What's wrong?"

Kady sat against her headboard, panting, coming down off a double adrenaline jolt.

"Poor baby, you have a nightmare?"

"Yeah. Just a nightmare."

Alana hugged her. "It's alright now."

"I'm fine, Mom," Kady said. "This thing with Luke, it's just shaken me up a bit."

"Of course it has," Alana cooed, getting up and sitting on the edge of the bed. "Course it has. You just don't worry about it. I'm sure he'll come back safe."

A quick frown passed over Kady's face. Alana saw it.

"What is it?"

"Mom, are you and Dad okay?"

Alana looked surprised. "What in heaven makes you think we're not?"

"You guys have just been. . ." she started, then stopped. Alana waited expectantly. Kady thought about whether she actually wanted to know the answer to the question she'd asked, but she decided she had to go on. She'd always been able to talk about anything with her mother. "You've been really weird ever since this thing with Luke. Like you've got something to tell me but you don't know how. Are you and Dad having trouble?"

Alana took her by the shoulders and looked at her hard. "Kady, listen to me. Your father and I are fine. We're not splitting up. We're just as much in love as ever."

Kady saw the certainty in her eyes, and felt suddenly bad for doubting her.

74

"Then what is it?"

"We're just *worried* about you, that's all," Alana said.

But that wasn't the answer. The conviction had drained from her gaze. There was something more, something *else*. They'd been edgy ever since Luke had disappeared. Pussyfooting around her, careful not to do anything to make her upset. When she went out, they always asked when she would be back. They'd never minded before. She'd caught her mother looking out between the curtains, watching the driveway at night, as if wistfully dreaming of home. Or as if she expected to see something there.

Alana was keeping a secret from her. And it hurt Kady deeply that her own mother would do that.

"Okay," she said, looking away.

"You go back to sleep, hmm?"

"I'm gonna read a bit first. Leave the light on."

"Sure, honey."

Once Alana had left, Kady got out of bed in her pyjamas. There was no way she was going back to sleep with the dregs of that nightmare still in her mind. She sat down at the computer with a sigh and booted it up. Maybe Jess was around. It would be late afternoon in San Francisco.

She sat and watched her Mac run through its startup sequence, thinking. Seth had left her house that evening with a grim expression that she hadn't liked. At least he'd taken that comic with him, though.

It *couldn't* have been Luke in the comic. Because that was just impossible. Because if boys just disappeared off the face of the earth and turned up inside a comic, hunted by horrors, then nothing in the world made sense any more.

Kady refused to believe it. Maybe the artist – what was his name, Grendel? Strange name, obviously not real – maybe the artist had just read about Luke in some local paper and used his picture as a model for a new character. But had Luke even *been* in the papers yet?

No. His mother hadn't wanted any publicity. Seth's parents had said so last time Kady was over at his house. Linda couldn't face dragging her grief into the spotlight, exposing herself to the hungry eyes of the media. Seth's dad had muttered about how selfish she was, putting her pride before her son's welfare. She should go on the news, let the public help. Seth said the news never helped anyone; people just liked to hear about bad things happening to other people. Naturally, an argument had followed. Kady had beat a hasty retreat.

The artist *couldn't* have known. Not this fast. It had only been two and a half weeks. Even if he'd started drawing the instant Luke disappeared, it would have been virtually superhuman to get a comic drawn, printed and in the shops within that time.

Her mind kept skipping back to the comic. The stories had weirded her out, and not only because of the content. They were chopped into sections, each of which was signed with the artist's name and the title of the comic. But the execution was oddly jerky. The sections would start halfway through a story and then cut away to another one, sometimes before the first had finished. Once, it returned to a storyline after some time had passed, and she had no idea what had happened in the interval.

They weren't really stories at all, she thought, just a chaos of incidents. Awful incidents.

She opened up her Instant Messenger, but Jess wasn't online. *Probably out having fun in the sun*, she thought. Then she remembered Jess lived in San Francisco. *Having fun in the fog, then*, she corrected herself.

She heard a long, low yowl from her wardrobe, and went cold.

A cat could sound a lot like a baby crying, when it had a mind to. It was one of the eeriest sounds Kady could imagine. She turned and looked at the door to her wardrobe. It was a beechwood IKEA model. Her father might have been rich, but he didn't waste money on wardrobes.

It's just Marlowe, she thought to herself. *He fell asleep in the wardrobe and I shut him in.*

So why wasn't she getting up?

Because it didn't *sound* like Marlowe.

She sat there staring at the wardrobe door. Why was she so creeped out? This whole Malice thing was getting to her. If she didn't watch out, she'd start believing it the way Seth believed it.

But that would mean that she'd just seen one of her best friends killed by some godawful shadow-beasts, and she wouldn't*wouldn't*WOULDN'T believe *that*.

There was a scratching noise from the wardrobe.

Regular, patient. Something wanting to be let out.

She got up from her seat, hesitated, and walked slowly over. There was another slow, menacing yowl, the sound of a cat at bay, as if it were warning away a dog.

"Hey, Marlowe," she cooed. "Hey you. You in there?"

Of course he's in there, what else would be?

She reached out. Her hand closed around the handle of the wardrobe.

Don'topenthedoordon'topentheDOOR!

She pulled it open.

And there was her cat, a streak of silver fur with black stripes, darting out between her legs and pouncing up on to the bed. In one smooth motion he sped from the cupboard to the warm hollow in the bed left by her body, and curled up there.

"You gave me a fright, you dumb moggy," she told him. *Moggy* was her favourite bit of English slang she'd picked up since she'd got here. Marlowe narrowed his eyes and looked smug.

"What were you doing in there, anyway?" she asked him, peering into the cupboard. In the bottom corner, beneath the hanging clothes, was a stack of old magazines and bits of correspondence, one of many similar piles she had lying around the house. She was a terrible hoarder, and very sentimental. She hung on to all kinds of junk simply because it was connected to some memory, as with that strange little ornament on her bookshelf, the tentacled creature encircling the cloudy egg.

Marlowe had been into this pile and scattered it all around. She started picking up magazines, which she'd collected because they had pictures of some singer she'd had a crush on. She couldn't imagine why she'd liked him now. There were old letters from friends and a scrapbook with dried and crushed flowers.

Then she spotted the newspaper. She picked it out, stood up and stared at it. It was a copy of the London *Metro*, a free paper they handed out on the street in the capital. Dated over a year ago, not long before she'd gone to San Fran. It must have been packed in with everything else when they moved from London to Hathern, though she had no idea why she hadn't just thrown it out.

Why'd I keep this?

She struggled to remember. God, she could be such a scatterbrain sometimes. She was always forgetting everything.

Absently, she flicked through it, searching for a clue. It would drive her mad all night if she didn't solve this little riddle.

The answer came very quickly, but all it did was provide more questions. On page six there was an article circled in marker pen. She read it once, quickly, her amazement growing with every line. Then she went back and read it again.

She turned round and looked at Marlowe. Marlowe looked back at her.

"You know anything about this, cat?" she asked him.

But the cat, if he knew, wasn't answering.

ABDUCTION BOY

POLICE IN KETTERING, NORTHANTS CONCERNING THE STRANGE CASE

On April 19th **Henry Galesworth (13)** and brother **Ben (15)** went missing without trace from their parents' house.

More than 100,000 British teenagers run away from home or go missing every year, and at first the case of the Galesworths seemed no more remarkable than any other.

But several days later, mother Kelly found Henry in the bedroom he shared with his brother. He was confused and scared, and unable to say how he had got there. When asked about the whereabouts of Ben, he said simply that he "couldn't remember".

Upon examination by police psychologists, it has been determined that Henry is suffering from amnesia, probably as a result of blocking out something traumatic that occurred during his absence,

"CAN'T REMEMBER"

ARE APPEALING FOR INFORMATION
OF A POSSIBLE DOUBLE ABDUCTION

Police are concerned that Ben Galesworth may be in some danger, and that Henry may know where he is, but as yet Henry is unable to remember anything that happened from the time when the two boys disappeared until the time he was found by his mother.

"Amnesia is a delicate condition," said police psychologist David Wain at a press conference yesterday.

"If we don't proceed carefully, we could cause irrevocable psychological damage. Whatever has happened to this boy, it obviously been a terrible ordeal."

But he acknowledged that time was a factor, and pledged to do all he could to find out what secrets are locked in Henry's memory.

"I'm very aware that another boy's life may be at stake here," he said.

Henry Galesworth

1

It didn't take long to find Henry Galesworth's house. There was only one Galesworth family in Kettering. Kady ran a search on the Internet, planned a route on a mapping site, and the next morning she and Seth were on a train. Kettering was only forty-five minutes away from Loughborough. This time Kady paid for them both out of her own pocket.

The house was an unremarkable suburban semi-detached; a new-built, square building of bright red brick, lacking any character whatsoever. Across a busy road was a small park, though Seth thought it would be more accurate to just call it a field, as it was bare except for a few benches and some pointless concrete paths. There was no children's play area, no trees, no landscaped gardens. It was like someone had started to build a park and given up halfway through.

Seth sat watching some kids play football, using their backpacks for goalposts. It was another hot day, and bees droned from flower to flower on the roadside verges. Kady was sitting next to him, looking across at the house. A red Escort was parked in the drive.

Despite the drowsy heat, he felt anything but relaxed. The events of recent days had shaken up his world. He'd never have imagined, at the start of the summer, that he'd be playing the investigator like this. He felt like he was being swept along in something, and he was being rapidly taken out of his depth. It frightened and excited him at the same time.

"We should just go up and ask," he said. They'd been there an hour now.

"Ask what? 'Excuse me, Mrs Galesworth, we'd just like to ask your traumatized son a few things? Oh, by the way, did the other one ever come back? No? Shame.'"

"It just doesn't feel . . . I dunno . . . *honest*."

"Listen, this probably won't even be anything. If an army of psychologists couldn't get him to remember, you think we can?"

"They didn't ask the right questions," Seth said. He laid his hand absently on his satchel. Their copy of Malice was inside.

Kady sighed, seeing that there was no movement from the house. She looked at her watch. "Okay. If nobody comes out by three, we'll knock. You can deal with the mother, though."

Seth looked over at her. She was swinging her legs off the bench, blonde pigtails dazzling in the sunlight, a beanie hat on her head despite the heat. She wore baggy trousers and outsize shoes, a stripy T-shirt, a bead necklace and an array of straps and bracelets on her thin wrists. She dressed the way she lived: carefree, casual, expressive. Seth had liked her from the moment he first met her.

He'd been down at the BMX track with Luke and a few others. It was a section of humpy ground that one of them had discovered in some nearby woods. Over time it had been sculpted by unknown hands into a set of jumps, dips and banks perfect for bikes. The boys had claimed it for their own.

One morning, during the Easter holidays, they'd been riding the track when Kady appeared on a bike of her own. Without a word or an invitation, she went plunging in. She did pretty well, until she got to the jump they called the Devil's Elbow, on account of the blind left turn you had to take as soon as you landed. She didn't know the trick of it, and she careened into a dirt wall.

Seth had been following her on her run. He skidded to a halt, reached down, helped her up. Dirty-faced, she'd grinned at him.

"Not bad," he said. "Want to go again?"

They fell easily into friendship. She liked his recklessness and he liked the freedom that he felt when he looked at her. Perhaps it was because she was American, he didn't know; he hadn't met any others, except her mother. But he could never imagine her turning into one of the Dead like his parents. She was too flighty to be caged. She would be an actress, or a journalist covering exotic locations, or the wife of someone glitzy.

When on one occasion he said as much to her, she cracked up. Then, seeing that he was offended, she kissed him swiftly on the cheek. "You're sweet, Sir Knight."

He'd never quite worked out what she meant by that, but he'd never forgotten it either.

Kady noticed him looking at her, and gave him a puzzled smile. "What?"

"Nothing," he said. Then he became grave. "What do you really think happened to Luke?"

Kady's smile faded. She stared down at the ground. "I don't know. All I know is that there's something going on here, and we need to find out what." She glanced over at the house again. "I mean, that paper. Seth, what was that paper even doing there? I don't remember buying it. And I certainly don't remember circling that article in marker pen. So who put it there? Who's leaving us clues?"

Seth didn't know. But the incident with the newspaper had only confirmed his suspicions that there were forces at play here which he didn't understand.

He couldn't stop thinking about Luke. Was he really gone? Was it possible that he was never coming back? Just to think about it made something twist sharply inside him. But he'd never been a crier. He bottled it all up, letting pain turn to poison in his guts. That was just his way.

If Luke was dead, someone, somewhere was going to pay. He swore it, bitterly.

"Hey!" Kady said. "We got action!"

Someone was coming out of the house. As they watched, a middle-aged woman emerged. She was overweight, with long, lank brown hair in an unflattering centre parting. She went to the car, opened the door, and then said something to a pudgy teenager who was standing in the doorway.

"That's our boy," Kady said. "She's leaving him alone."

"What about the dad?"

"You see another car in the drive?"

They waited until the car was out of sight and Henry had gone inside again; then they crossed the road and went up the driveway to the house. Kady reached for the doorbell, then stopped.

"Once we get in there, let me do my stuff, right?" she said.

"Right."

"I mean it, Seth. Whatever you hear, you don't interrupt. You could really screw him up."

Seth nodded. He was feeling less and less certain about this, but it was the best lead they had. Whoever had left that newspaper in Kady's room had meant them to find this boy.

A sense of nervous anticipation grew inside him as Kady rang the doorbell. The door was opened by the same boy they'd seen earlier: short, pasty-faced, with greasy hair and a dull-eyed expression.

"Um . . . can I help?"

"Are you Henry Galesworth?" Kady asked.

He thought about that for a moment. "Yes."

"We need to talk to you."

"Oh," he said. He stared at them. "Are you Jehovah's Witnesses?"

Kady exchanged a glance with Seth. This one clearly wasn't the sharpest tool in the box.

"We're not Jehovah's Witnesses," she said patiently. "It's about your brother."

Henry looked suddenly distressed. "Nope! Oh, no way! Nope! Mum said not to talk to you people. She doesn't want no more journalists."

"Do we look like journalists?" Kady asked.

"Dunno," he said, after studying them a little.

"We're too young for journalists," Seth said. "Don't you reckon?"

"Yeah, s'pose," said Henry. "So what are you?"

"We just want to know some things," Kady said.

"Like what?"

Kady made a motion to Seth. He removed his satchel and pulled out the copy of Malice in its black wax-paper sheath. Kady took it from him and offered it to Henry.

"Ever seen anything like this?" she asked as she did so.

She didn't really need an answer. Henry wailed and fell back from the doorway, tripping over his feet and falling in a heap in the hall.

"Keep that away from me!"

"Have you ever seen anything like it?" Kady demanded. To Seth's surprise, she was stepping in through the door, brandishing it like a weapon.

"I don't know!" he cried, cringing. "Yes! Maybe! I don't know!"

She gave the comic to Seth to put away. Henry didn't relax until it was back in the satchel. Kady offered her hand to him and he struggled to his feet.

"Let us help you," she said.

Henry sniffled, head hung. "Alright."

2

"Okay, Henry. Now imagine there is a bucket at your feet. Imagine all your tensions draining away into that bucket, from the top of your head, out through your toes. Can you do that?"

Henry nodded, nestled in an armchair. His eyes were closed. The curtains had been drawn to dim the light in the living room. Kady sat opposite him while Seth occupied a sofa nearby, listening to her slow, relaxing monotone. They evidently hadn't opened the windows in here all day, and the combination of the stuffy heat and Kady's voice was making him sleepy.

"You're going to take ten deep breaths. Deep, deep breaths. I'll count them for you. One . . . two . . . three. . ."

Henry did as he was told. The breaths got deeper and slower as he got towards ten.

"Now imagine you're at the top of a flight of stairs. You're going to take a walk down those steps to the landing at the bottom. There are ten steps. With each step, you will feel more relaxed."

Henry half-nodded again.

"Now slowly walk

down the stairs.

One . . . two . . .

three. . ."

Seth felt his own eyes drooping. He had to shake himself and focus.

"Now you've reached the landing. There are ten more steps to the next landing. Down we go. One ... two ... three..." By the time they got to the bottom, Henry's breathing was very deep and slow.

Kady often sat in on Alana's hypnotism sessions, watching her mother work. Alana, pleased to have an eager apprentice, had shown her a thing or two. She'd obviously improved since the last time she tried to hypnotize Seth.

"Can you hear me, Henry?" Kady asked.

At first, he said nothing. Then he stirred and gave a drowsy grunt. "Yeah."

"You're very relaxed. You're in a safe place, Henry. Nothing can hurt you where you are."

"Yeah."

"Now I want you to remember. I want you to go back. Go back to the last night that you and your brother were in this house together."

"Okay."

"Do you remember what you were doing that night?"

"We had fish finger sandwiches. I put too much tomato sauce on mine. I couldn't taste the fish."

"Good, Henry. What did you do afterwards?"

"We went up to my room. I wanted to show Ben something."

"What did you want to show him?"

Henry didn't reply.

"Nothing can hurt you here, Henry. Was it a comic?"

Henry nodded. Kady glanced at Seth.

"A comic called Malice?"

He nodded again.

"And what happened next?"

Henry shifted uneasily. "I said, let's say the words."

"What words?"

"You have to say them six times."

Kady was about to ask her question again when she caught Seth shaking his head at her. Seth knew the words, alright. He also knew that nothing would persuade Henry to speak them again.

"So you both said the words?"

"Yeah. We got the things first, though. I'd collected them before."

"What things?"

"The black feather, the twig, the cat fur, the tear. I had to squeeze a spot on my nose. It always brings tears to my eyes. Then we put in our hair and we burned it and said the words."

"Then what happened?"

"We heard things. Noises." Henry's face creased into a frown. He was getting distressed.

"What kind of noises?"

"Like scratching, like . . . little feet." He flinched sideways in the chair, but his eyes stayed shut. "He comes when you're alone. He waited till we'd gone to bed."

"*Who* waited?"

90

Henry had begun to tremble. "*Him.*"

"You're perfectly relaxed, Henry. Nothing can hurt you in this place. What happened afterwards?"

Henry jerked in the chair again. He shook his head violently. Beads of sweat glistened near his hairline and on his upper lip.

"You can remember, Henry. You're among friends and nothing can hurt you."

Henry's whole body juddered. He was shaking his head, making a strange noise, a trapped word in his mouth: "*Nnnnnnnnn. . .*"

"You can remember!" Kady said, more insistently.

Seth was getting worried now. He knew enough about hypnotism to understand its dangers. You could really mess someone up if you didn't do it right. Kady was pushing too hard.

He opened his mouth to protest, but Kady held out her hand, one finger raised: *Shut it.*

"You can remember, Henry," she said. "Nothing's stopping you. Tell us what happened!"

Seth was still trying to decide whether to intervene, but he'd heard Kady's warning about interrupting a hypnotism. It was like waking up a sleepwalker. Bad idea. But he couldn't sit by and watch as Henry thrashed, in torment, forced to remember whatever terrible thing had happened.

Then he heard the sound of tyres crunching on gravel. He got up and went to the window, opened the curtains a fraction.

There was a car in the drive. Henry's mother was back.

"Kady. . ."

"I know," she said. "Henry! You have to tell us *now*!"

"*The dark!*" Henry cried suddenly, eyes flying open. But he wasn't seeing the living room of his house. His whole body had gone stiff, and he was looking about wildly, eyes unfocused. "It's so dark! Ben, where's your light? My light's going out!"

"Where are you, Henry?" Kady tried to ask, but he didn't seem to hear.

"Ben, I can hear them coming. Run! *Run!* Ben, watch out for. . . *Ben! Ben!*"

Henry's mother was out of the car now, and she could hear Henry yelling from inside. Seth watched as she slammed the door and came rushing towards the house, fumbling with her keys.

"Where's Ben, Henry?"

"He fell!" Henry shrieked, tears running down his face. "He fell in the dark and they got him! Oh no, oh nonono! I can hear them *chewing* him!"

"Kady!" Seth shouted. "You have to stop this!"

"Not yet!" she snapped. "I need to know! I *need* to!"

Her face was almost savage. Seth was taken aback by the tone in her voice. He hadn't realized how strong her feelings were about this. He'd thought she didn't believe him about Malice, but in that moment he saw that she was desperately afraid. Afraid it might be true. Afraid they were tangled up in some deadly game that she didn't know the rules to.

She needed answers. Whatever the cost.

A key was scratching in the lock. Seth heard the *clunk* of the bolt. He felt suddenly trapped, unable to act.

"Where are you now?" Kady demanded of Henry.

He was trembling, his face a picture of terror. "There's stars . . . stars underground. . ." he said, his voice faint. "The lady wants to shoot out the stars! Follow the eyes! Follow the eyes!"

"What lady? Who is the lady?"

The front door flew open, and Henry's mother came hurrying down the hallway. "Henry? Henry, are you alright?"

Henry suddenly lunged out of the chair and grabbed Kady by the forearm, staring intensely at her. His voice, when he spoke, was a frightened whisper.

"*The bells bring the beast.*"

Then he began to scream.

Henry's mother burst into the room as Kady pulled away from him. Henry was screaming at the top of his lungs.

"Who are you?" his mother shrieked at Kady and Seth. "What have you done to him?" She stumbled over to Henry, put her arms round him. "Henry, it's Mummy! Henry, what's wrong?"

Kady was backing off. Seth was paralysed. Henry's mother turned her face to Kady, blazing hate in her eyes.

"*What have you done to him?*"

They ran.

Rats in the Attic

1

From: Seth Harper <sethb4dishonour@v21.co.uk>

Subject:

Date: 24th August 2008 00:41:32 GMT+00:00

To: Kady Blake <kadybug@gmail.com>

Hi Kady. I'm writing this on my dads computer. You know how much I love e-mail (sarcastic) but if I call you your going to try and stop me doing what I'm going to do and if I write you a letter it'd take too long or it might get lost. This is too important to muck up. Anyway, I figure your in bed now so you won't read this till the morning. I suppose I could write a note and leave it in my room but then mum might find it or dad (god forbid). There's no way I'd tell them. They wouldn't get it.

I'm going to do the ritual tonight. I know its probably stupid and I'll be alright in the morning, you'll read this email and laugh. But you said you need to know and so do I. I've got to prove it. They say some kids make it out, I mean I've got a chance, I'm pretty athletic or whatever. But it's stupid trying to find clues when the only way to be sure is to just do it.

I feel so bad about what we did to that kid. Whatever this thing is it's ruining peoples lives. You saw Luke's mum, and that kids mum. I can't just do nothing. I know that man in the shop is something to do with it and you have to go there if I disappear. I don't know why somebody would make this comic but theres an artist (Grendel) and theres a publisher (Black Dice, just like the comic shop, its printed on the cover but of course no address.) Thats probably how they find the shop though, I can just imagine that guy like a drug pusher or something, like "Try this comic." Watch out for him though, I think he could be dangerous.

I can't go on not knowing. If I'm not here in the morning then Malice is real and that means Luke is dead. Its weird, I think I should be sad but its not sadness, its making me angry. We have to stop it happening again. I know you think I'm old fashoined or something but theres something going on and its not right and we have to do something aboutit. I'll try and come back as quick as I can, we can tell people or track Grendel down or whatever.

I'm just rambling now. I think I'm just putting it off. I have to do it, that's all.

95

Okay, one last thing. I might be being totally dumbo but I might be right, and if I am then I'm heading for the kind of trouble I might not get out of. If you can get your hands on some new issues of the comic, you'll see me again maybe, but I won't see you. But if I don't see you again, I just have to say that you are the coolest girl I ever met and I wish I'd known you longer.

Well I'm sure you'll read this tomorrow and nothing will have happened and you'll rip me to bits about what I just said, so I'd better go. At least one way or another we'll know the truth by then.

Catch you later (god I hope so, anyway)

Sir Knight

2

Once the email was sent, Seth turned off the computer and crept upstairs to the bathroom. His parents were long asleep, but Seth felt wide awake. He was scared and fired up all at once. It was the same hanging-off-a-cliff feeling he'd had that day in the Peak District. The day before Luke disappeared.

The bathroom was squeaky-clean as always, tiled in pale green with floral patterns around the edges. There was a shower cubicle at the far end, next to a frosted-glass window, a white toilet, a large sink. Above the sink was a mirror and several mirrored cabinets, reflecting Seth from half a dozen angles. The light in here seemed too bright. He was aware of the night outside, the darkness, pressing to get in.

He shut the bathroom door and locked it. His bedroom didn't have a lock (Dad wouldn't allow it) and he needed privacy for what he was about to do.

One way or another, we'll know the truth.

He took out the stone mixing bowl and the ingredients for the ritual from the towel cupboard where he'd stashed them. The bowl he'd brought from the kitchen; the rest he'd gathered from here and there. It was easy enough to find a black feather in the woods, since it was thickly populated by crows. The twig was even more simple. Cat fur wasn't. He thought of getting it from Kady's cat, but Marlowe was short-haired and didn't seem to shed at all. Eventually he went to a friend of his mum's who had a farm on the edge of the village. They kept cats to hunt mice. He asked them for some sheddings, saying it was for a summer art project. They were happy to oblige, and he went away with a golf-ball-sized hank of assorted fluff.

The tear was harder. He couldn't make himself cry. Even thinking about Luke didn't help. Eventually he went and chopped onions until his eyes hurt enough to squeeze a tear into a glass.

Sitting on the floor of the bathroom, he carefully placed the ingredients into the centre of the bowl. The order was important: black feather, twig, cat fur, tear. Then he clipped a little of his hair with scissors and put that in. Finally he used the cigarette lighter. The cat fur took up the flame eagerly, and the room filled with the stink of burning.

"Tall Jake, take me away."

Was it really possible? Could there be a whole other world, a place where there were no supermarkets, no daytime TV, no constant barrage of advertisements, spam emails, telesales?

"Tall Jake, take me away."

A new world, an unexplored land. No matter that it was full of horrors. If it even *existed*, that meant there was an alternative to *this*. A world of fakes and phonies, of politicians lying through their teeth and being allowed to get away with it. A world where anything that seemed too good to be true always was.

"Tall Jake, take me away."

People treated each other like dirt, the very skies were being poisoned while nobody did anything, hundreds of thousands were murdered in other lands while governments stood by and watched, communication was so easy that nobody *communicated* any more.

"Tall Jake, take me away."

And God help him, he realized he *wanted* to go to Malice. He realized he *wanted* it to be true. Because if this was real, then *anything* could be real, and that meant there was more than this world. New frontiers, unexplored lands. Maybe there was a place for him there.

"Tall Jake, take me away."

He was saying the words on automatic now. Faster, louder, because if he stopped now he might never find the courage to start again.

Anyone, take me away. Take me anywhere.

"Tall Jake, take me away!"

And it was done, almost before he'd knew he said it. Too late to take it back. His pulse was racing, but he felt suddenly chilly. Smoke curled up from the burnt mess in the bowl. The fire diminished to a smoulder, and went out.

He looked around, half-expecting to see a dark figure standing at the other end of the bathroom. But there was nobody there. The seconds ticked onward, as they always had.

He waited. Listening. Watching. His senses strained for a clue, a warning as to what might happen to him.

But nothing did.

After a time, he began to feel slightly ridiculous. He sighed, got up and opened the window to let out the smell. As an afterthought, he ran the bowl under the tap to be sure the fire was out, then took up the soggy wad and flushed it down the toilet. The mixing bowl was a little blackened, but it would scrub out. He put it down and leaned against the edge of the sink.

I should've known it was just a story.

The light in the bathroom stuttered. Seth's heart jumped. Darkness threatened for a few moments, then the light stabilized.

Seth held his breath.

"Come on," he said defiantly. "Come on, if you're coming."

Through the ceiling he heard a scuttling noise. A tiny clicking of claws, like rats in the attic.

Is this what you heard, Luke? Right before he got you?

He was freezing cold, and the air had a strange taste to it, as if he'd bitten his lip and tasted blood. Tinny, salty. The walls of the bathroom felt like they were closing in on him.

Suddenly his bravado seemed feeble. He'd been hasty. He didn't want to meet Tall Jake. He didn't want this. He could have tried to solve this from the outside, without going into Malice. He didn't have to stir up the forces that had taken Luke. He should have been patient, he shouldn't have acted without thinking.

Something was coming for him.

He got up, and caught sight of himself in the mirrors above the sink. Six wide-eyed faces stared back. For a moment, he didn't recognize himself.

The light flickered again, flashing from darkness to light.

There!

He spun around, but there was nobody. He released a shuddering breath. He'd *seen*. Just for an instant, in one of the mirrors. He'd seen someone standing in front of the door to the shower cubicle. Someone very tall.

There was a knock at the door.

Seth jumped, recoiled from the sound. The light stopped flickering.

"Seth?" said his mother. "Are you okay?"

Seth had never opened a door so fast. His mother was standing there, hair mussed and wearing a dressing gown. Ordinary, boring, *safe*. Her being here had somehow broken the spell. The sense of impending terror was fading like a bad dream.

"Who were you talking to in there?" she said, peering past him.

"I was on the phone," he said, with a weak smile. "Somebody called me while I was in the bathroom."

"At this time?"

He shrugged. "Yeah."

She sniffed. "Smells like burning hair in here."

Seth put on a bewildered look. "Might be someone burning leaves out in the field," he said. "The window's open."

She was tired enough not to pursue it any more. She yawned, and he thought how old she looked. He'd never noticed before.

"Sorry for waking you," he said.

She waved it away. "It's fine. What are you doing up, anyway?"

"Couldn't sleep."

"You want me to make you something? A hot malt drink will help you drop off."

The simple kindness of that made his heart hurt. In

that instant, he wished more than anything he could tell her about what he'd done. He wished he could let her know about Malice. He wished he could assure her that he wasn't running away (although maybe he really was), that none of this was her fault, that she'd done the best she knew how to.

He wished he could tell her, but she just wouldn't get it.

Seized by an impulse, he hugged her. And even though he hardly ever touched her, she hugged him back as if it was the most natural thing in the world.

"I'm sorry, Mum," he said quietly. "I'm sorry for being such a pain. You deserved better than me."

"Seth!" she said. "Don't ever talk that way. I'm very proud of you. So's your dad, though he wouldn't ever say it. What's brought this on?"

"I dunno, Mum. Maybe I'm just tired."

She stepped back, brushed back his hair and felt his forehead to see if he was ill. So typical of her: she meant well, but she always got it wrong.

"You should get to sleep. You want that drink?"

"I'm okay. I think I'll just go to bed."

"Alright. Night night, then."

"Night."

He went along the landing and back to his room, closed the door quietly behind him.

"Goodbye, Mum," he said quietly.

He understood it now. It must have happened this way

with Luke. Luke's mum must have interrupted the process, just like Seth's mum had. So Tall Jake came back later. In Luke's case, it was the next night.

The chant was only a request. An invitation. Tall Jake would come when he was ready. It might be tonight, it might be tomorrow. Might be a week, might be never. But if he wanted you, if he *chose* you to play his horrible little game, he'd come when you were alone.

The immediate threat seemed to have faded, but Seth wasn't fooled. He'd invited the darkness in. It was only a matter of time.

He turned out the light and lay down on the bed, still fully clothed. Suddenly, he was exhausted. The stress and fear had worn him out.

His eyes drifted closed and jerked open again. He hadn't drawn down the blind, and bright moonlight shone through the window. The wiry aerials of nearby houses cut up the skyline.

It's done now, he thought, and there was something oddly peaceful about that feeling. He'd set himself on a course and there was no changing it.

Suddenly he thought of Kady. She would get that email tomorrow, call him frantically and find him safe and well. He'd never convince her about what he'd felt tonight, and he was embarrassed about the things he'd admitted to her. But at least he'd been honest. Honesty was important to him.

His eyes drifted closed, snapped open once more.

There was a tall, dark figure standing in front of the window.

3

At 2.22 a.m. Seth's mobile began to ring on the bedside table. The display lit up green, casting an eerie light into the room. The caller ID said KADY.

It rang out and went to answerphone. A few moments later it rang again, and once more went unanswered. Eventually it stopped, and silence returned.

In the distance, a cat yowled plaintively in the night.

THE CLOCK TOWER

An Unpleasant Delivery

1

"I'm Justin, by the way," said the boy, as he squatted down next to the mechanical thing that only moments ago had been trying to kill Seth. He produced a screwdriver from a pocket of his hoodie and began levering open a small panel on its back.

"Seth," Seth heard himself say, as if introductions were the most normal thing in the world under the circumstances. But nothing was normal any more. His brain felt fogged with impossibilities. The train, the metal creature at Justin's feet, the girl . . . the dead girl. . .

He'd heard her scream. The last noise she ever made. By the time he got to her, it was too late.

Something like panic was waiting, lurking in the dark places of Seth's mind. At any moment, it might rush out and overwhelm him. This *couldn't* be real, it just wasn't *logical*, it must be a *hallucination*. Maybe he was living an elaborate dream. Maybe he'd been hypnotized and this was all someone's idea of a joke.

But his senses knew the truth. He could smell the oily reek of the pipes; he could hear huge cogs grinding away behind the walls; he could feel the bruises left by the creature's fingers on his shoulders, and the weight of the wrench in his hand.

Tall Jake had taken him away, alright. And put him here.

"What *is* that thing?" he heard himself asking.

"This? It's a Chitter. Least, that's what we call 'em, 'cause of the noise they make." Justin had opened the panel on the Chitter's back by now. Inside was what appeared to be a shard of crystal, about six inches long, held in a metal cradle. Justin slid it out, examined it a moment, then put it in his pocket.

"There was a girl. . ."

"I heard."

"We should *do* something, I dunno. . ." he trailed off.

"Where is she?"

Seth took him around the corner, where the skeleton of the girl lay. She was nothing more than a clutter of bones now, inside a pile of dirty clothes. Justin squatted down next to the skeleton. He sighed and shook his head sadly; then he reached down and picked up a silver bracelet that loosely encircled an arm bone.

"You knew her?" Seth asked. He had to look away: he couldn't face the sight of the dead girl any more.

"Yeah." Justin was rummaging through a small knapsack. After a moment, he drew out a large white ticket. It looked like an admission ticket to a carnival ride. "You did it, Tatyana," he murmured to himself. "You did it."

Something clanked in the distance, echoing down the corridor. Justin looked up sharply, then stuffed the ticket in his pocket and stood.

"Come on," he said. "It's not safe here."

Without waiting for an answer, he went back to where the shattered Chitter lay. Seth followed, not knowing what else to do.

"You're pretty handy with that wrench," Justin said. "Keep an eye out. I'll carry this guy." And with that, he squatted down and lifted the Chitter with a grunt. It was the size of a child. "These things weigh a ton," he said through gritted teeth, then set off down the corridor. Seth trailed after.

"We're just going to leave that girl there?" Seth asked. "Shouldn't we, I dunno, bury her or something?"

"What's the point? She's dead."

"Isn't that *usually* when you bury people?"

Justin looked back at him, his face grim. "Listen, mate. You're new, so let me give you a tip. Don't get sentimental. You're here to *survive*. Forget about everything else." He gave Seth a bitter smile. "Welcome to Malice."

2

The air tasted of oil. The corridors were dense with pipes and vents, cogs and gears. The walls were covered in a thin layer of grime, and the sound of hidden machinery came from everywhere. Justin huffed and hurried through the maze of corridors, carrying his heavy burden, and Seth kept pace with the wrench held ready to swing at anything that might spring out.

"What happened to that girl?" he asked.

"Tatyana."

"Tatyana. I mean . . . it sucked her dry."

"Close. It sucked all the *time* out of her."

"It did *what*?"

Justin looked round a corner, determined it was safe, and motioned Seth onward with his head.

"Those things, they drink time. There was one poor guy, he was fifteen. Chitter got him. By the time they pulled it off, he was eighty."

"What happened to him?"

"Would *you* want to live like that?" Justin asked. "He walked into the Menagerie, never came back."

Seth opened his mouth to ask what the Menagerie was, but Justin intercepted the question. "Look, I'll give you the tour when I get a chance, but right now I got bigger things to worry about. Like how I'm gonna tell Tatyana's boyfriend about this."

"She had a boyfriend? How long has she been here?"

"Not sure. Hard to keep track. Anyway, they came together," said Justin; then he laughed. "Stupid, right? We live inside a great big clock and nobody ever knows the time. Now shut up and keep your eyes peeled, huh? There could be more of those things around."

Seth was too heartsick to take offence. He did as he was told, checking gloomy corners as they went. Overhead lights fizzed and stuttered fitfully. There were dozens of places where something the size of a Chitter could hide, and the constant, restless noise of machinery made it hard to listen out for them. He became more and more paranoid as Justin led him onward, and soon he was jumping at shadows.

Eventually they reached a metal door at the end of a short corridor. Justin kicked it a couple of times.

"What's the password?" came a voice from behind the door.

"Har har," said Justin. "Hilarious. It's me, you idiot. Let me in."

There was the sound of bolts being drawn and then the door opened. A thin, unhealthy-looking teenager with patchy blond stubble and a dirty face peered out. He spotted the Chitter in Justin's arms, then Seth behind him.

"You had a busy trip," the boy commented.

"Dan, meet Seth," he said. "Seth, Dan. Now get out of my way, this thing's giving me a hernia."

He pushed on in and Seth followed. Dan shut and bolted the door behind them.

Behind the door was a dingy and featureless stone room, with doorways leading into other, similar rooms. Some of them were hung with ragged curtains for privacy. The corners were piled with junk and debris: bits of boxes, scrappy blankets, some metal bowls. It smelled bad in here, like old sweat.

Through one of the doorways he could see a half-dozen people clustered around a small fire which burned in a wire box in the centre of the room. Almost all of them were teenagers, though he saw one kid who couldn't have been more than ten. He was huddled up against a narrow-faced girl, who stared blandly at Seth.

"Home sweet home," Justin muttered. "It's not much, but at least the Chitters can't get to you here. The only way in or out is through that door."

They passed through another room before reaching one which was evidently being used as a workshop. There were parts scattered everywhere: cogs, gears, pistons. Devices and machines lay in various states of construction or disassembly. Seth saw a brass arm and hand, a tiny mechanical bird, and some kind of mini-vehicle that looked like a Meccano kit gone horribly wrong.

Justin dumped the Chitter unceremoniously on the floor, then groaned and stretched, putting his hand to his back.

"How many people are here?" Seth asked.

"Ten of us. You'd make eleven, if you stayed." His tone made it clear that he didn't really care either way. "People come and go. Sooner or later, some of them want to try to get out of here."

"And how *do* you get out of here?"

"Same way you came in. By train."

"What, you mean you can just get on and leave?"

"Not without a ticket. Did you read Malice at *all* before you decided to say the chant?" He gave Seth an exasperated glare, then folded his arms and studied him closely. "No, wait; I bet you were one of those kids who just did it for a dare. You look like the sort."

Seth didn't rise to it. "It's a long story."

"Well, anyway. I'll keep it basic for you. Malice is divided into different zones. The Deadhouse, the Oubliette, the Labyrinth, the Terminus, so on and so on. They call them *domains*. In each domain there's a few ways to get out, but—"

"What do you mean, out? Out where?"

"Out. Home. Back to family and friends and school and all that. Anyhow, one way out is to get yourself a ticket. Without one, the Conductor won't take you."

"I met him," Seth said.

"Creepy, ain't he? Well, there's two types of ticket: black and white. A black ticket buys you one trip anywhere within Malice. To a different domain, say. A white ticket buys you one trip anywhere at all. Even back home, if that's what you want."

"You mean some people don't?"

Justin shrugged again. "Some kids have been here for years. Some kids don't *want* to go back."

Seth recalled how he'd felt when he was saying the chant in his bathroom. How he'd actually wanted to come to Malice. But that was before he knew. That was before he realized what he was really asking for. He'd just seen a girl turn into a skeleton right in front of him.

Then he remembered what Justin had taken from her knapsack.

"She had a white ticket, didn't she?"

"That's not for you," he said sharply.

Seth raised his hands, palms out. "Just asking."

Justin relaxed a little. "Sorry," he mumbled. "I liked Tatyana. Didn't know her all that well or anything, 'cause they only got here recently, but . . . y'know. . ." He scratched the back of his neck, looking awkward. "Thing is, she'd want me to give it to Colm. She was really, y'know . . . in love with him and stuff. More than he was with her. She was just one of those emotional types, I think."

"Sure, of course," Seth said, but Justin went on talking.

"See, Colm didn't have the guts to go into the Menagerie. He was too scared by what he'd seen since he came to Malice. But she wouldn't take it lying down. She said she'd find him a ticket, get him out of here. Then she'd go and get another one for herself." He took the white ticket out of his pocket and stared at it. "This one was for him."

Seth was thinking of the teens he'd seen around the little fire. This place oozed desperation and hopelessness. Those kids were hiding, huddled in miserable safety, terrified of what lay outside. Prisoners of their own fear.

"The train's stopped," he murmured.

Justin looked up. "What?"

"The train. It's being held at the station. Nobody's going anywhere with or without a ticket." He suddenly grinned, out of nowhere. "This place isn't so different from home after all. Trains never run on time there, either."

Justin stared at him in surprise, then barked a short laugh. "A sense of humour! Thank Christ! Hang on to that, mate. You're gonna need it." He leaned in closer, as if there was somebody nearby to hear. "Take it from me. This place can crack you. Stay smart, keep on your toes, don't get too attached to anyone. Now tell me exactly what you heard."

"Just what the Conductor said. He said there'd been an incident."

"You didn't ask what *kind* of incident?"

"I'd only just woken up in Malice," Seth said. "Wasn't feeling too sharp, what with all of reality being turned upside down and that."

Justin grunted. "Did you see the clock, then?"

"The one above the archway? Yeah."

"Was it running?"

Seth frowned. He remembered noticing it when the doors of the train first opened, and again later, after his conversation with the Conductor. He'd thought at the time that something was odd.

"I don't reckon so," he said. "Couldn't be sure, but I think it had stopped."

Justin was smiling. "I bet it was Havoc. I just bet it was them." He caught himself, looked over at Seth, groaned. "Now you're gonna ask me who Havoc are, right?"

"I was thinking about it."

"Look, I've been where you are. Take it one thing at a time, huh? First thing you need to know is where you are. How the Clock Tower works, all that stuff. Otherwise you'll get dead pretty quick. But first –" he held up the white ticket – "I got an unpleasant delivery to make."

"I'll come with you," said Seth. "I was the last one to see her. I should . . . well, I should probably come."

Justin shrugged. "Suit yourself."

3

They found Colm in the room where the fire was burning. He was playing a game of chess with himself, using screws and stones as the pieces, on a board made of squares scratched into the stone floor. A large fan in the ceiling beat the air slowly, sucking away the smoke from the blaze through a vent. The light of the fire mixed uneasily with the electric lights on the walls. Dan was holding a metal bowl above the flames, using a pair of pliers so as not to burn his hands. Inside was a vile-looking brown mush.

Justin didn't bother to introduce Seth to the room, and nobody introduced themselves. The other kids looked tired and hungry, and they regarded him without much interest. What struck him as strange was that most of them didn't seem to be *doing* anything. Just sitting there, staring into the fire or slumped against the wall. They had the air of the condemned about them.

Colm was a little more animated. He was underfed and he had dark rings around his eyes, but he had a roguish grin and a lively manner that set him apart from the others.

"My man Justin!" he said in a thick Irish accent. "And who's this you bring with you?"

"I'm Seth. You're Colm, right?"

"Ah! My reputation precedes me even beyond this godawful hole you find yourself in. Colm it is. You got the look of a new boy about you."

"Just in, fresh off the train," Seth said.

"And how d'you like your holiday so far, Seth?"

Seth looked around the room. "I got lied to by the brochure."

Colm burst out laughing at that. "I don't suppose on your travels you came across a ravishin' young lass, Russian extraction, name of Tatyana?"

Seth couldn't hide the reaction on his face. Colm's smile faded. He looked at Justin, whose expression was grim.

"What is it? Out with it now. What you come to tell me?"

Justin produced the bracelet that he'd taken from the skeleton's wrist, and held it out to Colm. Colm stared at it, then at Justin.

"We found her," Justin said.

Colm took the bracelet slowly. The other kids in the room, knowing what Justin meant, were quietly getting up and leaving.

"Where?" Colm said at last.

"In the corridors. I think she was on her way back from the Menagerie." He looked away. "She got caught by a Chitter."

Colm had the bracelet held in his hands. He seemed stunned. Unable to think.

Justin held out the ticket. "She had this on her. Reckon it was for you."

Colm had tears shimmering in his eyes. "I should've been with her. I should've gone."

When Colm showed no sign of taking the ticket, Justin pressed it into his hand, next to the bracelet. Colm barely noticed.

"I'm sorry, girl," Colm whispered. "I should've been with you."

His grief was hurting Seth to watch, but he felt he had to say something.

"We killed the thing that got her," he said. "But I . . . I was too late."

"Did you get the crystal?" Colm demanded, suddenly.

Seth looked confused. "The what?"

"The crystal!"

"I got it," said Justin. He drew out the crystal shard from a pocket. Colm snatched it from him. He clutched it in both hands, glaring at it furiously; then he burst into tears.

Seth and Justin retreated as unobtrusively as they could, leaving him alone. Seth was relieved to get out of there.

There was nothing worse than seeing another boy cry. The other kids had moved to another room. He could hear their voices murmuring behind one of the curtains that hung across the doorways.

"What's with the crystal?" he asked Justin, as they headed back to the workshop room.

"Okay, this is how it works," Justin replied. "The Chitters hunt us down here. When they catch somebody, they suck the time out of them and store it in those crystals. The crystals are what provide the life for the Timekeeper's automatons in the Menagerie. We know because some kids saw the Timekeeper actually putting one in, and the thing came to life right after."

"They fuel these . . . automatons with time they steal from the kids?"

"That's about the size of it."

Seth just accepted it. There wasn't anything else he could do. "So what does Colm want with that crystal?"

"It's kind of a rumour. They say when someone is drained, there's still something of them left inside the crystal. Like, a piece of their minds or their souls or whatever. Me, I think it's just wishful thinking. They just wanna believe that some part of their dead friends live on."

Seth felt himself overwhelmed by a terrible fear. It came on him suddenly, as if a dam inside had burst, unleashing a tide of horror to swamp him. Malice was real, and he was living it. People died in here. Real people, dying for real. Everything he'd ever known had fallen to pieces, and he wanted to fall to pieces with it. He wanted to scream or cry or go berserk, anything to let out the pressure he felt inside.

But it wouldn't do any good.

You did this, Seth. You asked for it.

"You don't look too hot," Justin said.

"I've had a rough morning," Seth replied.

Justin slapped him on the shoulder in sympathy. "Just forget what you think you know. There's more surprises in store yet."

"Easy as that, huh? Forget everything."

"Easy as that," Justin grinned. "You're a survivor. I can tell straight off. Give yourself a bit of time to find your feet. You'll be alright."

"I'll never stay in here," said Seth. "I won't live like this. Trapped."

"Mate, you ain't seen the half of what's out there. Might be you change your mind when you've had a look at the Menagerie."

Swill

1

Seth sat in a corner of the workshop, among the junk, and thought. He thought about what he'd done. He thought about the things he'd given up when he decided he just *had* to know the truth about Malice (but wasn't that just the way he was? He couldn't help it). He thought about his mum, and the last conversation they'd had, and how she'd be heartbroken when he was gone in the morning and probably blame herself. Dad would mutter about how they'd raised such an irresponsible child, while secretly he would be worried sick.

Forget them for the moment, he told himself. *You've got bigger problems now.*

And so did Kady. Because Malice was *real* (he had to keep telling himself that, over and over). She would get his email, and she would know the truth. That meant she would be going to London again, back to the shop. But Seth was suddenly afraid that the shopkeeper was much, much more dangerous than they'd thought.

He was selling these comics. He was sending kids to this terrible place (well, no, strictly speaking they were sending *themselves*). But *why*?

Malice was real. That meant what had happened to Luke was real. He'd seen his best friend devoured by those shadow-things.

Luke was gone. Really gone. And he wasn't coming back.

Just to think it felt like a blade twisting in his stomach.

It seemed like hours that he sat there. Justin was tinkering with the Chitter that they'd salvaged, poking around inside it with a set of weird-looking metal tools. "If there's one thing we're not short of down here, it's tools," he'd told Seth earlier. Then he'd gone on to say how, apart from attacking kids and turning them into skeletons, the Chitters also serviced the delicate mechanisms down here. These were the maintenance corridors beneath the Menagerie, Justin said, and all the cogs and gears were part of the unbelievably complex clockwork system that operated in the floors above them.

People came in and out to ask about Tatyana. Justin told them what he saw, and also that the clocks had stopped. The visitors didn't show much reaction. It was all the same to them whether the clocks were running or not. They weren't leaving this place.

Some of them glanced at Seth, perhaps thinking that he might have some interesting stories, a word of hope, news from outside. Anything to break up the endless boredom of hiding. But they saw the expression on his face, and left him alone.

Bit by bit, Seth imposed some order on to the chaos in his head, and the lurking panic receded. He forced himself to stop thinking about the world outside. That wasn't his problem any more. *This* place was his problem. This place, this *real* place.

He'd spent his whole life living with rules. Rules of behaviour, rules of life. It's dark at night and light in the daytime. Don't cross the road without looking both ways. Strangers can be dangerous. Eat with a knife and fork. It's sunny in summer (sometimes) and it's cold in winter. There's no such thing as monsters.

But Malice had new rules. Rules he *didn't* know.

Learn the world. Then you can beat it.

He held on to that. If he viewed this place as a challenge, he felt a little less helpless. There were ways to get out. All he had to do was find one.

"These things are incredible," Justin said to himself, as he took apart the delicate mechanisms in the Chitter's shoulder.

"What?" Seth said, stirring.

"You're alive, then," Justin observed. "Thought you'd slipped into a coma over there."

"I'm still here." He stretched. He'd gone stiff from sitting so long. "Working things out."

"You get anywhere?"

"Well, I don't feel I'm going to go insane any time soon. That's an improvement on before."

"That's the spirit. Soon have you naturalized." He tapped the Chitter with the end of a screwdriver. "I could work on these things for ever and not understand half of what goes on inside them. It's a sealed clockwork system that winds itself when they move. And don't get me started on the brain. There ain't *nothing* like this back home."

"They're powered by dead teenagers," Seth said. "In case you forgot."

"Well, yeah," he said, scratching the side of his neck with the tip of the screwdriver. "I can see how people might have a problem with that."

Seth got to his feet and went over to get a better look at what Justin was doing. He was trying to work this kid out. Did he talk that way because he genuinely didn't care, or was he covering something up? His accent was rough; even when he was being friendly he sounded aggressive. Though physically he was small and scrawny, he made up for it in attitude.

"You're quite the mechanic," Seth observed.

Justin shrugged.

"So how'd you end up in here?"

Justin didn't reply.

"Don't want to talk about it, then. Okay."

"This place is like prison, mate," Justin said. "You don't ask people what they're in for. They tell you if they feel like it."

"Is that how it is in prison?" Seth asked.

Justin gave him a poisonous look, then resumed examining the insides of the Chitter. "Three months in borstal. Don't ask what for unless you want a split lip."

"What for?" Seth asked immediately.

"What did I just say?" Justin demanded angrily, throwing the screwdriver aside and standing up to face Seth.

"What you *said*," Seth replied, voice steady and even, "was a threat. Don't you threaten me unless you mean to do something about it."

Some distant part of Seth, the little voice of reason, was asking him why he got himself into these situations. Why he was picking a fight with the boy who was the closest thing he had to a friend in here. But he wasn't one to back down from a confrontation. And someone threatening to hit him, whoever it was . . . well, he wouldn't just sit there and take it. It wasn't in his nature.

Justin glared at him. Seth was bigger, but he suspected that Justin would attack someone twice his size with the right provocation.

But Justin smiled instead. Grudgingly, but he smiled. "You're alright," he said, and the tension went out of the room. "Most of these kids, they don't have any guts. Still hoping Mum and Dad are gonna appear, or someone's gonna save them or something. Tatyana, she had guts. You'd've liked her."

Dan appeared in the doorway, interrupting the wary moment of respect between the two of them. "Hey, new kid! Food run. You're up."

"I just got here!" Seth protested.

"You wanna eat, you go get food. Justin, you wanna go with him?"

"Yeah, why not?" Justin replied. "He'll only get himself killed otherwise."

"Wow," said Seth, with just a tinge of sarcasm. "I'm looking forward to this already."

2

"There it is," said Justin.

Seth looked into the gloom. From the doorway where they stood, a single railed walkway projected across a shaft towards a metal column in the centre. The column came from the ceiling high above and disappeared into darkness below. A few meagre electric lights flickered and stuttered on the walls of the shaft.

Seth was holding the wrench that he'd used to club the Chitter with. He scanned for signs of any more of them. It felt dangerously exposed here.

"Keep an eye out," Justin said. They were hidden in the shadows of the doorway, but enough light fell on his face for Seth to see his grim expression. "This is where they get you. They know we have to come to get food and water, so they lie in wait."

"You mean they *provide* the food and water?"

"That's right."

"Why?"

"I told you. The Timekeeper needs kids to give life to his little toys. Makes sense to keep us alive until he wants us. There's no other food down here."

"Just enough to stop you starving, right?" Seth said, with disgust in his voice. He was thinking of the malnourished faces he'd seen earlier. Justin didn't exactly look healthy, but he wasn't too bad; maybe he hadn't been here so long, or maybe it was because he hadn't given up hope yet.

"I'll not lie to you, mate," Justin said. "It's about as nutritious as diarrhoea and only half as tasty. If you heat it up it's almost bearable, but finding stuff to burn ain't that easy. To get anything useful – blankets, wood, whatever – you have to go up to the Menagerie." He snorted. "Everything's a pain round here."

We're like mice, running around inside some giant machine, Seth thought. *Scavenging what we can, hiding from the cat.*

"Looks clear," said Justin.

They hurried out on to the walkway, each carrying a large tin bucket. At the far end the walkway widened into a platform, on which was a small metal trough and a little stack of bowls. Above the trough was a chute that projected from the column, with a lever next to it.

"Grub's up!" said Justin, and pulled the lever. A thick brown slime, mixed with white lumps, oozed out of the chute and began plopping into the trough.

Seth eyed the nauseating mixture. "Suddenly feels like I'm back in the school canteen."

"Don't it just?" Justin asked with a grin. "We call it *swill*. Though I don't think even pigs would eat it, given the choice."

Seth bent down and sniffed, then recoiled. The trough smelt like a yak had used it as a latrine, and later as a mausoleum. "Jesus!"

"Come on," said Justin. "Grab a bucket."

They filled the buckets from the trough and Justin shut off the lever. "Get yourself a bowl too. They're provided by the management. Might as well take advantage."

Seth took a bowl and stuck it in his bucket, where it was sucked down by the ooze. They hefted their cargo of slop and headed back along the walkway.

"Hey," said Seth as he passed beneath the doorway and into the corridors. He turned around to look at Justin. "Isn't there any way to—"

They heard a soft mechanical noise from above.

Chittachittachitta

"Look out!" Justin shouted. Seth caught a fleeting glimpse of two burning blue eyes among the shadowy pipes, and then the Chitter launched itself at him. It crashed into his chest, gripping his shoulders with strong fingers, knocking him to the ground with its weight.

Seth frantically pushed it away as it lunged for his throat with its hypodermic teeth. Somehow he got the wrench in between them and jammed it into the Chitter's mouth. It began to screech, scrabbling at him, its head darting back and forth to get a clear bite. He kept the wrench firmly stuck in its mouth, panic lending him strength. He'd seen what had happened to Tatyana.

Don't let it bite you!

Justin swung his bucket of swill into the Chitter with a crash, knocking it off Seth's chest and spraying slop everywhere. The wrench flew free from Seth's hand and skidded into a corner.

The Chitter sprang to its feet, animal-fast, and crouched to attack its new foe. Its clockwork tail lashed the air.

Justin backed up along the walkway, out into the shaft, towards the column where the swill came from.

"Anything you wanna do, do it now!" he said to Seth, never taking his eyes from the creature. It was advancing on him, walking on all fours in a monkey-like prowl.

Seth looked around desperately for the wrench. There! He got up and ran for it, but he was too slow. The Chitter leaped at Justin, straight for his chest. Justin caught it as it came. There was a moment of furious screeching and pummelling, and then Justin turned and flung it over the side of the walkway. Its mechanical squeal lasted only a few seconds before it hit the ground far below.

Seth joined Justin at the walkway rail, looking down into the darkness of the shaft.

"Ow," said Justin. "That must've hurt."

Seth started to laugh with slightly hysterical relief. "I think you spilled some swill on me," he said, pulling out his T-shirt to show where he'd been splattered with it.

"Mate, you are *never* getting that out," Justin said.

Then the two of them cracked up, and for the first time since he got here Seth felt like himself again.

3

Despite their close encounter, Justin insisted that they detour to the train platform once they'd refilled the bucket of swill.

Seth didn't complain. He'd had a scare, and there was no doubt that the Chitters were very dangerous, but they'd destroyed two of them now, and Seth was feeling a little more confident. They were fast, but they were small, and they could be beaten. The new bruises on his shoulders were beginning to ache along with the old ones from the last attack, but if bruises were the worst he'd come off with, then he could count himself lucky.

The train was still in the station, its doors closed. They stayed only long enough to confirm that the clock above the entrance archway had indeed stopped, and then they were on their way again.

"What's so important about the clock?" Seth asked as they hurried back to safety.

"This is the Clock Tower, right?" Justin said. "It don't just keep track of time, it *runs* time. This place runs the time in Malice. Take it from me: till those clocks start again, the sun don't set and the moon don't rise. The whole land's in lockdown."

"Havoc?"

"Maybe," he said. "Probably. My guess is they did

something to the railway, so the Timekeeper stopped the clock till they can fix it. Stop the clock, you stop the trains running."

"What *is* Havoc?"

"It's a bunch of kids like us, out there in Malice somewhere. Screwing things up. Breaking stuff, sabotaging the system, smashing whatever." Seth didn't miss the admiration in his tone. "They don't take no guff from nobody. They make TJ sorry he ever brought 'em here."

"TJ?"

"Tall Jake."

Seth grinned. Tall Jake had terrified the wits out of him last night. Hearing his name casually mocked made things a little less scary. And hearing about Havoc gave him a valuable shred of hope. Maybe this wasn't an impossible situation after all. If Havoc could get away with causing all kinds of problems, then there were certainly other ways to exist in this place that didn't involve hiding in fear.

"So the trains won't run till the clocks start again?" he said.

"*Now* you're getting it. The trains run on a schedule. They ain't never late, arriving *or* departing. So till that clock reaches the right time, that train ain't leaving that station."

"You know a lot about it," Seth observed.

"I read Malice for a year before I said the chant. Got a few tips."

"A year?" Seth said. "How long's the comic been going, then?"

"Dunno," Justin replied. "It's anyone's guess. Few years, I'd say. Three or four."

Four years? Seth thought. *How many kids have come through here in that time? How many like Luke?*

The thought of that appalled him. Somebody had to do something. *He* had to do something.

4

They got back to the hideaway to find it in a state of unrest.

"Colm's flipped his lid!" Dan said as he let them in. They didn't need him to tell them that. They could hear Colm's anguished cries already.

Justin pushed past him and Seth followed. They dumped their buckets of swill on the floor and headed towards the source of the sound. Several kids were clustered around a curtained doorway, listening with a kind of frightened curiosity. Colm was swearing and yelling within, his voice hoarse. As they neared there was an avalanche of crashes as a pile of metal bowls was thrown aside. One of them skidded beneath the curtain, past Justin's feet.

They went on in. The room was a ruin. Colm had thrown about what meagre furniture he could find – bedrolls and bowls and a couple of pots. One of the pipes that ran along the wall was dented.

Colm's hair was wet with sweat and tangled, his lips

skinned back from his teeth. He was clutching the crystal shard in one fist, panting. For Seth, the smell of the hideaway was overwhelming in here: unhealthy, unwashed bodies, festering in an enclosed space. He imagined that Justin didn't even notice it any more.

"Hey! Hey! Calm down!" Justin said as they entered.

"I let her go out there to *die*!" Colm howled. "She died 'cause of me!"

"No, she didn't," Justin told him. "She died 'cause of this place. She was just trying to get out, same as all of us."

"I should've gone with her!" he shouted, and kicked a bowl into the wall with a loud clatter.

"Colm, this isn't doing any good," Seth said. "You think she'd want this?"

"And who're *you* when you're at home, eh?" Colm demanded. "You didn't even *know* Tatyana!"

"It's 'cause of him that you have that crystal, and that bracelet, *and* that ticket," said Justin. "If it weren't for him she'd have died for nothing."

Colm glared at Seth through the hair that hung across his face, trying to decide if he was friend or enemy. Then he turned his attention to Justin.

"I gotta get out of here," he said. "I got my ticket. I gotta get out. It's what she'd have wanted."

"That's right, mate," said Justin. "Soon as the trains are running."

"That could be weeks! It could be months! You don't know when, do you?"

"No," said Justin, whose patience was getting a little thin. "I *don't* know. So just sit tight and wait."

Colm shook his head wildly. "We gotta start the clocks."

"You what?"

"The clocks! We go up past the Menagerie, up to where the Timekeeper is, and we—"

"You need to calm it down a bit, Colm."

"Come with me!" he pleaded, grabbing Justin by the front of his grey hooded zip top.

"Get off!" Justin cried, shoving him away. Colm staggered back, tripped and fell heavily.

"I'll go," Seth said quietly.

Colm fixed on him like a drowning man to a lifebelt. "What'd you say?"

Seth raised his head. Louder, he said: "I'll go with you."

"*He'll* go with me!" Colm crowed at Justin, thrusting a finger at Seth.

"You don't know what you're doing," Justin said to Seth.

But Seth *did* know. Colm's wild grief had unnerved him. He was afraid that if he didn't keep on moving forward, then the black, hungry feeling that had been snapping at his heels might catch up with him. The feeling that had been getting closer ever since he came to Malice; ever since he realized that Luke was gone for good.

"I know what happens if I stay," he said. "Getting weaker and weaker eating that slop. Hiding away. Pretty soon I'll have no spirit left to fight. I'll be like those kids out there. Just waiting for someone to save me."

"Rather die on your feet than live on your knees, eh?" said Justin.

"Something like that. You said you can get tickets in the Menagerie?"

"Sure, there's ways. They're hidden on the upper levels. You never really know where. You just have to look."

"Then I'm getting myself a ticket and I'm getting out of here. I'm gonna stop this, somehow. All of this."

Justin snorted. "Good luck trying, mate."

Colm had got to his feet and was making a half-hearted attempt at dusting himself down. He gazed at Justin expectantly.

Justin gave a long-suffering sigh. "Do either of you have any clue how to start a clock as complicated as this one? Anyone have the first idea about pawls, winding rotors, ratchets?"

Seth and Colm looked at one another, then both grinned. Justin groaned.

"Fine," he said. "Let's do it. Anything's better than another eating another bowl of that godawful swill."

A Name for the Cat

1

It was a hot, close day heading towards a warm, stuffy night, and Kady was hiding behind a garden wall in London.

The house the garden belonged to was unoccupied, left to spiders and shadows. The five-foot-high wall was leaning and all that was left of its gate were some rusted hinges. The garden had run to weeds and nettles, which reached almost to the height of the wall.

On the opposite side of the road, a little way down the street, beneath a railway arch, stood Black Dice Comics.

Kady itched in the heat, worsening an already bad mood. Midges danced in frantic clouds in the air, and she was sure things were crawling into her shoes. She'd had plenty of time to think while she'd been waiting here, watching the door of the comic shop through the gate. Plenty of time to get good and furious.

How could he *do* that to her? How could he just go off without her? To take a risk like that? Weren't they friends? Weren't they in this together?

144

And now he was gone, and he'd left her alone.

I know that man in the shop is something to do with it and you have to go there if I disappear, he'd said, in that email he'd sent. Why didn't he just talk to her first? Why was he always so reckless? Of course she'd have tried to talk him out of it. That was what he was avoiding. And she'd have been *right* to do so, because now . . . now. . .

Seth had gone to Malice. It didn't seem possible, but unless he was playing some kind of monstrous joke on her, that was the only explanation.

Last night, she'd woken from a horrible dream; the same one as the night before, with the cowled thing and the flamethrower. She'd turned on her computer and seen the email from Seth. She hadn't slept a wink the rest of the night. When he didn't answer his phone, she knew. He was gone.

In the morning she told her parents she was going to a friend's house in Leicester. She put on her kooky little backpack and hiked across the fields to Loughborough to catch the train to London. She had to do it today, before it got too late. Before Seth was missed and the police started calling and everyone got suspicious. First Luke, now Seth? With the paranoid way her parents had been acting, they'd never let her out of their sight again.

Plus, she needed to do something. She would go crazy if she sat around at home, turning it over and over in her head. She was furious at Seth, but beneath it all she was scared to death. What if the same thing was happening to him as happened to Luke?

She hung on to her outrage and her sense of betrayal instead. It was just easier to be angry than frightened.

She checked the clock on her mobile. It was a little past six. She'd been watching for hours, and nobody had entered or left the shop. They certainly didn't do very brisk business. But then, this wasn't the kind of place that would advertise. This was a place kids had to *find*. It would take a rumour, a whisper, a clue to bring them to this dingy shop with its weird shopkeeper. And maybe, if he felt like it, he'd tell you about a new kind of comic called Malice. A *secret* comic. Because didn't all kids love secrets?

Kady shrank back into hiding as the door to the shop opened and the hulking shopkeeper came out. Despite the heat, he was wearing a trench coat and a grey fedora. It was the kind of hat Kady imagined a Chicago gangster wearing in the thirties. The trench coat barely fit over his massive shoulders. He locked up the shop and then headed down the street, away from Kady.

Kady waited a little, then followed.

She had no idea that tailing someone could be so nerve-wracking, or so hard. She'd pictured herself darting from cover to cover, staying out of sight, but in reality there was very little cover on an empty street. The garages were still open, but that just made it worse, because the mechanics could see her. She would look ridiculous – and *very* suspicious – hiding behind postboxes and railway arches all the way up the street.

But there was one thing in her favour. People just didn't

look back very often. So she trailed after the shopkeeper, her head down, keeping her distance. She'd read somewhere that people could sense when they were being stared at, so she only glanced at him every now and then. She tried to hug the corners so she could get out of sight if necessary, but really, she knew it was hopeless. If he turned around, he'd see her. He'd wait for her to catch up, maybe. He'd ask her what she was doing, in that horrible, high-pitched, breathy voice of his. And then . . . then what? She didn't know. She didn't want to find out.

But he didn't look back.

She followed him towards the train station, where there were more people. She relaxed a little once she had a few commuters between them. He was easy to keep track of, because he was half a foot taller than everyone else. She kept that gangster's hat in sight as the traffic got thicker.

The shopkeeper took the train to Waterloo, changed to the Jubilee Line for Westminster, then changed again for the District Line to Kensington Olympia. Kady shadowed him every step of the way. She almost lost him twice in the sweaty crush of people on the tube, but each time his size and that distinctive fedora gave him away before he slipped out of view.

By the time they got to Kensington it was getting towards dusk. Sunset came late at the end of August, around eight o'clock, but the journey had taken more than an hour and the sun was now a sultry red behind the terraces. Kady was just glad to be able to breathe again. The tube in summer was appallingly hot. She remembered reading once about how it was illegal to transport cattle at that temperature, but it was apparently okay for humans. It had been funny then.

The shopkeeper headed through a brick arch, down an alley into a row of mews houses hidden from the street. Sensing that they were nearing the end, Kady peeked around the corner of the alley in time to see him standing in front of a door. It was opened for him by a strict-looking lady with pointed, sharp features, and blonde hair tied back in a severe bun.

They exchanged a few words – loud enough so Kady could hear her prim English accent – and the shopkeeper went inside. The lady turned to follow, then stopped, a suspicious look on her face. Her eyes narrowed, and she surveyed the street. Kady pulled her head back quickly, to avoid being seen. For a few moments there was silence; then she heard the door close.

She leaned against the alley wall. Now she had an address.

The next part would have to wait for nightfall.

2

She retreated to a café where she could keep an eye on the entrance to the alley. There she bought a coffee and thought about what she had to do next. She ran through possibilities and threw them all away, until she was left with only one.

She had to get into that house.

Calling the police was useless. She could imagine her story. *Please, Mr Policeman, my friend has been abducted by a character in a comic. Evidence? Oh no, sir. I do have this blank comic I can show you, though.*

Go straight to nuthouse, do not pass Go, do not collect £200.

She thought about other things she could do. Follow the shopkeeper more? Observe from a distance? But time was running out. As soon as the news broke that Seth was gone she'd be grounded. And big as their house was, it wasn't the kind with a convenient tree outside her bedroom window that she could climb down to sneak away.

No. She had to do it now.

She was scared. Really scared. Being a private eye wasn't half as much fun as she'd been led to believe. She called her dad and spun him a story about how she was at a café in Leicester with her friends and she'd be back late. Greg was less likely to get excitable than Alana, who would no doubt demand her immediate return.

"You make sure you stay with your friends, sweetheart," Greg said. She could hear the worry in his tone. "I'll come pick you up when you're ready."

"I will, Dad. Thanks."

She hung up. She didn't have Seth's conscience. Lying wasn't a problem for her. Not if they were little white lies like that.

By the time the café closed, the streetlights were on and the city was as dark as it would get. She had to get this done or she would miss her train back north. The idea of being stuck in London at night made her feel sick with worry. Not to mention her parents' reaction. Even her easy-going stepfather would go berserk if she had to call him to come get her.

Get on with it, then.

She crept down the alley, to the hidden street of mews houses: a secluded row of tall, narrow buildings, steeped in the yellow glow of the city. Some of them were occupied. She spotted the one the shopkeeper had gone into. Lights were on inside.

She moved closer to the house. Number 6. There was a gate at the side, leading down a narrow alley to the back. Gingerly, she tried it. Locked. But there was a gap between the arch and the top of the gate. Not very big, but probably big enough for, say, a certain American girl with a surplus of curiosity.

She looked around. Nothing moved, but no matter how many times she checked, she couldn't convince herself that nobody could see her. At any moment, she expected to feel a hand on her shoulder, a deep voice saying, *'Ello, 'ello, 'ello? What's all this then?*

Since she hadn't had much experience with them, her idea of British policemen was stuck somewhere in the fifties, when they all had moustaches and very tall hats. She feared that *'Ello, 'ello, 'ello?* far more than the bored drawl of a California cop. Nobody could make "hello" sound sinister like the Brits could.

She took off her pack, passed it through the gate and then

climbed over. It was a squeeze, and for one panicky moment she thought she'd got stuck, but she wriggled herself loose with a scrape and a bump. She scooped up her pack and headed down the narrow alley to the rear of the house.

It was dark here, away from the streetlights, which made her feel safer. The back yard was small and paved. There was a clay trough full of dry soil pushed against one wall. The plants within had browned in the recent heatwave, and were now wilting in the stifling, windless night. Other houses crowded close to overlook the garden, but there were no lights on in any of the facing windows.

There were lights on in *this* house, however. Kady crept up to one of the windows and peered inside.

Only curtains. They were shut tight. Not even a crack to see through. But she could hear voices, too muffled to make out. She tried the other window. Probably the kitchen. The result was the same. A blind had been pulled down, and she couldn't see through.

She went to the back door, listened, and very slowly pushed the handle down.

Something brushed against her leg.

She almost screamed, her hand flying to her mouth.

A black tomcat sat there, looking up at her. It mewled appealingly, as if to ask: *What are you doing? Can I play too?*

Kady let out a slow breath, counting to ten to allow all her murderous desires towards that helpless animal to subside.

"Cat," she whispered. "I'm kinda busy here."

She tried the back door again, but it was locked. She stepped back, frustrated. The fact that she couldn't get in should have given her great relief, but now she was here, she found that she hated the idea of going away empty-handed. She studied the house, thinking.

The cat meowed again, drawing her attention. It was rubbing itself against a big iron drainpipe. Kady followed the drainpipe with her eyes. On the second floor (*first* floor, she reminded herself, since she'd lived in England long enough to know) there was a sash window, left half-open. Probably to provide ventilation in the muggy night.

She looked at the cat. The cat watched her expectantly.

"You have *got* to be kidding," she said.

3

The room at the top was a mess. It was dingy and smelled sour. A large double mattress lay next to one wall, a duvet rumpled up beside it, with sheets that looked like they'd never been within a mile of a washing machine. A big piece of wallpaper had come away, revealing a faded magnolia beneath, and speckles of mould haunted the upper corners of the room. A huge wardrobe stood in the corner, half-open and full of grey suits. There were open cans of Coke everywhere, but they congregated mostly around the bed.

By the smell, Kady was in no doubt that this was the shopkeeper's lair. But it had the sense of temporary lodgings.

This wasn't his home; it was just a place he was staying.

She stepped down from the sill and into the bedroom. The drainpipe was sturdy and had presented her with no problem at all. She'd always been a good climber. It was a weird talent to have. Alana used to joke that they'd injected her with monkey glands when she was a baby.

Experimentally, she looked in one of the Coke cans. It was half-full. She picked up another. That also had some left in it. After trying a couple more, she realized that none of them had been finished.

She wasn't sure exactly what it said about the shopkeeper's personality, but it creeped her out.

Lying in a corner, she spotted a copy of Malice. Unopened, still in its black wax seal. The red M was face down. She picked it up as if it were radioactive, holding it as far away from herself as possible, and quickly slipped it inside her pack. Her fingers felt cold and numb where she'd touched it, and her hand had pins and needles for a minute or so afterwards.

Beyond the door was a landing. The plaster on the walls was cracked and yellowing, and the threadbare pea-green carpet was coming up at the edges. To her right was another door and some stairs leading up the next floor. On her left were stairs going down. The house was tall and narrow, and the voices from below carried up to her. She padded over to the top of the stairs, where she could see down to the foyer, and listened. The owners of the voices were somewhere out of sight.

". . . not sure it is necessarily a good idea to move at this point," the woman was saying. She spoke in a very schoolmarmish tone, as if to a naughty child.

"It's time." This was the shopkeeper. "Two odious little malcontents came in a few days ago. The girl . . . I just got a feeling from her, something I couldn't place."

"Icarus Scratch, you're becoming paranoid."

"I'm a salesman, my dear Miss Benjamin. I can read people. Now the boy, that vile little robber, he *knew* something. I think he was *investigating*."

"If you are worried about them causing trouble, we can simply get rid of them."

"One of them has already taken himself out of the picture. The boy found his way into the latest issue. Unfortunately he's still alive in there."

Kady put her hand to her mouth.

Seth!

"And the other?"

"She's still at large. That makes her dangerous. I think they were on to us when they first came to my shop. Now her friend has disappeared, she'll be sure."

Kady shuddered in horror. If they knew that she was upstairs right now, listening to them. . .

But she had their names now. Icarus Scratch and Miss Benjamin. That was a start.

Something thumped softly behind the door of the other room, the one she'd not looked into. She frowned in puzzlement, but she was too interested in the conversation below to move.

154

"And how is Grendel?" Miss Benjamin was asking.

"Who knows what someone like that thinks? He's drawing, that's what's important."

"But he's not drawing the right *things*! What about showing us something useful? Like where Havoc's hideout is?"

Kady's ears pricked up. Havoc? What was that?

"Grendel draws what he sees," Scratch replied. "I can't help it if he doesn't stay on subject."

That was interesting. Kady had noticed before how the stories weren't really complete stories, but rather scenes from different parts of Malice that restlessly flicked back and forth. Sometimes they just showed random incidents, other times they would follow a kid in peril and then abruptly change to something else, as if the artist had got bored.

She wondered how much control they had over their comic, in the end. Maybe there was something there she could exploit.

There was another thump from behind the door. This time it was loud enough to demand investigation. She sneaked down the corridor a little way, and listened.

Something was moving in there.

"You should go back to Crouch Hollow." Miss Benjamin's voice came drifting up the stairs. "Perhaps you can try persuading him again. Havoc's latest little trick was the worst yet. They took down a whole section of the railway. We need to—"

- We need to increase circulation. -

The voice set Kady on edge like fingernails down a chalkboard. It made her think of rusted metal, stale ashtrays, empty tombs. A third person in the room. And Kady had no doubt at all that it was someone she didn't ever want to meet.

"No," said Scratch. "We do it carefully. Keep it a rumour. A rumour is more powerful. We give them something to believe in. And we make sure they keep it from their parents."

- Adults will not believe like children do. Why do you fear them? -

"Because sooner or later they will connect Malice to the missing children, and that could make things very hard for us. Why do you think we use an ink that fades over time on contact with air? So there's no *evidence*. Oh, people are stupid alright, but you get enough of them together and *one* of them might have a bright idea."

Of course! That was how it worked. Once the airtight wax paper was unsealed, the ink would fade after a few days. No wonder Luke's copy was blank. It meant you couldn't collect copies of Malice, or find back-issues. You bought a copy, you read it, and soon after it was gone.

Keep it a rumour. A rumour is more powerful.

Kady looked through the keyhole. The room beyond was dank and gloomy, and it seemed to be empty. She could see no bed, no furniture. But she'd definitely heard something.

*- This is your world, **Scratch**. I have no choice*

but to trust you. But I have enemies still, hidden or lost, and the time may come when they think to move against me. -

"This *is* my world, and without me there would be no comic at all," said Scratch, with an arrogant tone to his breathy girl-voice. "Remember that, Tall Jake."

Kady took her eye from the keyhole as she felt herself go cold. Tall Jake. Tall Jake was downstairs. Tall Jake was here, in this world, in *reality*.

Something heavy bumped against the door. She jumped in fright.

There was no further sound. She waited, her heart decelerating. Silence. She leaned closer, hesitated, then put her eye to the keyhole.

A slitted eye was looking back at her.

Kady only just managed to stop herself from screaming, but she couldn't stop herself lurching away from the door. She tripped and went over with a thump on the landing.

"What was that?" Miss Benjamin's voice was sharp.

"It was just the—" Scratch began, but she cut him off.

"Somebody is upstairs!" she hissed.

Kady moved. Across the corridor, into Scratch's bedroom. The carpet dampened her footsteps. She rushed to the window, already hearing somebody on the stairs.

At the last moment she changed her mind. She'd never get out of the window in time. They'd catch her before she could clamber down the drainpipe. Instead, she slipped into the wardrobe and pulled it closed, a moment before

Miss Benjamin appeared in the doorway.

Kady held her breath among the musty suits. There was a tiny crack between the wardrobe doors, through which she could see Miss Benjamin. Her heart was thumping hard enough to make her whole body tremble.

Miss Benjamin had that same suspicious expression on her face that Kady had seen when she opened the door to Scratch earlier. She scanned the room slowly.

Then she sniffed the air. Once, twice. Her head tilted up, like an animal scenting after prey. She sniffed the door jamb, all the way down. An awful smile spread across her face.

"Girl. . ." she said, almost to herself. "A young girl. . ."

Kady felt terror clutch at her throat. She wished more than anything that she'd gone out of that window, that she'd *thrown* herself out if she had to.

Miss Benjamin crouched low, sniffed at the floor. She took a step into the room, then another, sniffing all the way. She raised her head and looked directly at the wardrobe.

Miss Benjamin couldn't see her through that tiny crack. But she could *smell* her.

"Are you in there, girl?" she asked. "I think you are."

She took another step. Reached out for the wardrobe door. Kady willed herself to disappear, to be anywhere but here, and then—

There was a loud meow. Miss Benjamin froze, then spun around. There, in the corridor, was the black tomcat Kady had seen outside. It meowed again.

"A cat?" Miss Benjamin asked herself. "No, not just a cat. You're one of *hers*, aren't you?" She moved towards it, hunched over like a crone. "I know you. I know your name. *Andersen!*"

The cat arched its back and hissed. Miss Benjamin lunged, making a grab, but it bolted away along the corridor to the right. Miss Benjamin chased after it.

"You tell your queen to keep hiding! You tell her that!" she cried as she thundered up the stairs in pursuit.

Kady didn't think twice. She was out of the wardrobe, out of the window and down the drainpipe so fast that she almost fell off it. She dropped to the garden, fled to the gate, and was over and away long before Miss Benjamin came back and found that the wardrobe doors, which had previously been shut, were now hanging open.

The Menagerie

1

Seth couldn't believe his eyes.

Since he'd arrived here, he'd seen a monstrous train and its bizarre conductor; the nightmarish Chitters who drained time from their victims; the grim, dank maintenance corridors where terrified teenagers hid and ate swill to survive. He'd come to take it for granted that Malice was a kind of grimy hell, lit by dim electric lights.

But the Menagerie was a wonderland. A glittering carnival of glass and chrome, polished surfaces and bright colours. There were carousels with strange beasts that writhed and gaped as they moved. There were elaborate buildings like giant doll's houses, with gaudy figures acting out silent scenes within. A shiny train, its front end fashioned into a grinning face, chugged along upside down on an aerial track. The metal boughs of mechanical trees swayed in a small clockwork park, blown by an imaginary wind.

Even more amazing were the occupants of the Menagerie.

Many were animals, or creatures that resembled animals. Others were unlike anything Seth had ever seen. But all of them had been built, all made of cogs and gears and joints, unimaginably complex. There was one automaton fashioned like a giant ball, the height of a man, which rolled around studying the world with lens-like eyes that dotted its surface. A silver horse, sleek and elegant, nosed at the ribbons of a maypole. And overhead...

"Are those *birds*?" Seth asked.

They were crouched behind a candy-striped tent, near a small door that led back to the maintenance corridors. There was a much more grand entrance, apparently, but it was guarded by clockwork lions who were liable to maul them. This door, hidden away in a cluttered corner of the Menagerie, was how the kids below sneaked in and out.

Justin followed his gaze. The ceiling of the Menagerie was far, far above them. Stairways and paternosters led up to giant platforms, suspended from cables or fixed to the walls, where more attractions had been built by the Timekeeper. Between them, large winged shapes glided lazily through the air.

"Vultures," said Justin.

"That's impossible. Clockwork birds? They'd be too heavy to fly. It breaks the laws of physics."

"You remember what I told you before?"

It took Seth a moment to work it out, then he shook his head and smiled wryly. "Forget what you think you know," he said.

"Exactly."

Seth watched the birds. "Ah, the laws of physics were overrated anyway. No big loss."

"There it is," said Colm, pointing. "The lift. See it?"

Seth did see it. A thin golden tube heading straight up from one of the platforms, disappearing into the ceiling.

"That's our way up," he said. "Up to the Clock Tower."

Seth was getting an idea of the layout of this place now. Underground, there was the subway and the maintenance tunnels. Above them was this vast Menagerie, and above *that* was the tower itself, where the clock machinery was. And where the Timekeeper lived.

"What are those?" he said, indicating several large round holes in the roof leading to smooth tunnels of metal.

"That's how the Timekeeper goes back and forth," Justin told him. "Once he's built a new toy, he has to bring it down here to put it in the Menagerie. But he's too big to get into the maintenance tunnels. That's what the Chitters are for."

Justin had told Seth all about the Timekeeper. Seth had never been the imaginative sort, but the picture Justin painted in his head was still enough to worry him.

"Enough of that. Let's get goin'," said Colm. He hefted the length of lead pipe he'd brought with him. It had been sharpened at one end to a spear point. Justin had a similar weapon. Seth had brought the wrench. It seemed a pitiful defence against the kind of things that might be waiting for them, but it was the best they could do.

They crept into the Menagerie, skirting round the tent.

Seth couldn't help thinking it was laid out like an amusement park. All that was missing were the people. There were thoroughfares between the attractions, little pagodas and gazebos to rest in, drinking fountains that splashed and trickled with water. *Clear* water, not like the cloudy stuff they drank below, which they collected in buckets from dripping pipes.

"Don't trust it," said Justin, noticing Seth's interest in one of the fountains.

"It's poisonous?"

"Nobody knows," he said. "Nobody's wanted to find out."

Everything moved in the Menagerie. Things rotated, faces yawned and laughed, figures slid back and forth on tracks or emerged from little gates to strike a bell. As incredible as it all was, it made Seth uneasy. The faces, even the smiling ones, all had a dark edge to their expressions. They seemed wicked, or frightened, or sly.

And then there was the music, which drifted from the carousels and the dioramas. It was a little out of tune, just enough to set his teeth on edge. The competing melodies from different attractions clashed and became strange. The lullabies and carnival ditties that should have been comforting ended up sounding sinister.

Justin looked round a corner, then waved them into hiding. Seth and Colm crouched behind a merry-go-round ridden by clockwork children. A moment later the silver horse walked idly past, tossing its head and snorting.

"Is that thing dangerous?" Seth asked, after it had gone.

"Don't know," said Justin. "You can never tell. Some of them are violent, some don't seem to care. Best just avoid them altogether."

"They say it depends on the person," Colm added. "The person they used to give it life. If they were an angry sort, that there beast they're put into is angry too."

Justin gave Seth a look that indicated he didn't believe a word of it, but Colm spotted him.

"What about your man Vincent, eh?" he hissed. "What about him?"

"Vincent?"

"He was a nasty one," Justin muttered, scanning the thoroughfare ahead of them for signs of any more automatons. "Big kid with a bad temper. He couldn't stand that he was trapped here, took it out on everyone else. Me and him didn't see eye to eye."

Seth could imagine what that meant. Justin wasn't the kind to be pushed around.

"Chitters got him in the end," Colm said. "And not long after, we all start hearing about a new automaton in the Menagerie. Big ugly gorilla, mean as sin. I tell you, if that don't sound like Vincent, I don't know what does."

"Anyway," said Justin. "Vincent or not, we don't much want to run into that gorilla."

They made their way onward, looking for a way up to the higher platforms, where Justin had said the tickets were usually hidden. By staying off the thoroughfares and hiding behind the rides, they managed to avoid the attention of the bigger animals. They were spied by a shiny brass crab with pincers big enough to snap their bones, and once they came face to face with an enormous snake of segmented chrome, wrapped around the strut of a colourful water-tower. But neither of these animals seemed interested in them, and they were allowed to pass.

Seth was getting a bad feeling about all of this. Something told him that Colm was here for other reasons than the need to get the clock started. It didn't make sense to risk himself when he had a ticket out of Malice. Was it grief or guilt that sent him up here? The desire to prove to himself that he wasn't a coward after all? Or was it the Timekeeper he was after?

Then there was Justin. Seth didn't understand his angle at all. He didn't give the impression that he was trapped here like the others. He hadn't lost his spirit. Seth didn't know exactly why, but he thought that Justin was *waiting* for something. He sat and tinkered in his workshop and waited.

So what reason did Justin have to help them out? Why did he come? Seth would have asked, but Justin had made it clear that he didn't like questions about himself.

But he'd find out, one way or another.

His thoughts drifted to Kady. She was the reason that time was pressing on him, the reason he needed to get the clocks running, to get a ticket quickly. He'd left her in danger on the outside. He'd proved that Malice existed; now he needed to get out and do something about it. They needed to warn the world.

But why had nobody *else* done that? If Justin had been reading Malice for years, and if some kids escaped as everyone said they did, then why hadn't they gone to the papers? One kid might be called crazy, but dozens of them . . . well, it'd at least make for an article, right?

Unless. . .

He had a sudden, awful feeling that sucked all the wind out of him. He sat down, his back to a low wall that surrounded a lake of metal waves that rose and fell like the scenery of a bad theatre production.

"What on earth d'you think you're doing?" Colm demanded, hurrying back to him.

"I shouldn't have come here," Seth said. "I should've waited, I should've thought it through."

"Mate, this isn't the time," said Justin, reaching down to grab his arm.

Seth allowed himself to be helped up. "They're *all* like Henry Galesworth," he said.

"Your man's gone mad," Colm said impatiently.

"*Listen* to me!" Seth said. "I just realized something. I can't leave! You know why nobody talks about Malice after they get out? It's because they *don't remember*!"

Justin propelled him towards shelter, between a funhouse and a little Ferris wheel populated by clockwork children who waved and laughed as they went around.

"Look, this is fascinating and all, but unless you want us to die here, we ought to stop standing around in plain sight, yeah?"

They raced into the cover of the funhouse, where Seth leaned against the wall, his head still spinning.

"Now," said Justin. "Explain."

"We met a kid, Henry Galesworth. He'd been to Malice, but when he came back he couldn't remember where he'd been. He'd forgotten all about the comic. We thought it was just, well, you know, he'd repressed it or something. Like, he was so traumatized by what happened to his brother. But what if it wasn't that? What if *every* kid who comes back from Malice forgets where they've been? It's the only way the comic could stay secret so long."

"So when you get out of here, you don't remember a thing?" Colm asked, then sneered. "Suits me fine."

But he didn't understand. Neither of them did. It was all useless. No matter what Seth found out in here, he would be unable to take it to the outside, to get it to Kady. If he tried to leave this place, he'd just end up the way Henry did. He wouldn't be able to help Kady any more. He wouldn't be able to do anything about Black Dice or Grendel or the shopkeeper. He wouldn't be able to do anything to stop the people who made Malice, because as soon as he returned to his world, it was all over. His memories would be wiped as blank as the comic he found in Luke's room.

Idiot. As usual, he'd thrown himself into things. He

hadn't looked before he leapt. And now he was trapped here, because if he tried to leave, everything he found out in Malice would mean nothing.

That was Tall Jake's cruellest trick yet.

"Hey," said Justin, seeing the despair in his eyes. "Whatever you're thinking, don't. You give up in here and you're dead. You don't know nothing about this place. There's a whole *world* out there beyond the Clock Tower. Maybe you're right, maybe you're wrong, but even if you're right, well, we'll fix it." He grinned. "One thing I'm good at, it's fixing things."

Seth felt a surge of grateful warmth. At least he had an ally in here. No, more than that. In that moment he knew Justin was a friend. He didn't know what he'd done to deserve it, but he was thankful.

He opened his mouth to speak, but then he caught sight of what was behind Justin. Squatting on the spokes of the Ferris wheel, looking down at them with interest, were three clockwork mosquitoes. Each was the size of a small dog, made of gold and brass, with large, oval green eyes. Their noses – probosces, Seth vaguely remembered from biology – were thin, foot-long spikes, and their wings were made of some kind of transparent fibre veined with metal.

Justin saw his expression, looked over his shoulder. Colm went white.

"Hoof it!" Colm cried, and the three of them took to their heels.

2

They hadn't got far before the mosquitoes launched after them, their wings a blur as they whined through the air. Colm was in the lead, and they followed him, having no better direction to go. They raced along a path through a fairy landscape of giant mushrooms and peeping hobgoblins, glancing over their shoulders as the sound of the mosquitoes got louder and louder.

A change in the pitch of a mosquito's drone warned them as it dived down towards Colm. Justin put on a burst of speed, caught him up and pushed him an instant before the mosquito swooped. Both of them fell forward, and the mosquito swept over their heads, its sharp proboscis scraping the air.

Seth pulled Justin up as another mosquito dived. Colm lunged to his feet, swinging his lead pipe, and caught it square on the flank with a heavy blow. It shot past them and smashed into the ground, cogs and springs spilling everywhere.

"That's for my girl, you filthy bloodsuckers!" he shouted.

"Come on!" Justin said, breaking into a run again. "Get under cover!"

They left the path and headed into the shelter of the giant mushrooms, dodging between them as they went. The caps of the mushrooms afforded some meagre protection, at least. They could hear the angry whine of the remaining two mosquitoes overhead. Witches' huts and laughing pixies flashed past as they sprinted through the surreal fantasy world.

They'd just reached the edge of the fairyland when a mosquito came in low and straight at them. They threw themselves aside as it sliced past like a lance. Seth kept running, but suddenly he couldn't see the other two, who had disappeared somewhere in among the rocks and toadstools and enchanted trees.

He burst out into open ground. There before him was a carousel, playing an out-of-tune jingle as it turned. Beyond he could see a set of spiral stairs leading up to the higher levels.

He looked around frantically for the mosquitoes. One was nowhere to be seen; the other was circling above the fairyland attraction. It zeroed in on him and plunged down. He ran as fast as he could towards the only cover in sight: the carousel. No time to worry about the others. He could hear the mosquito getting closer, faster, descending like a divebombing fighter plane in an old World War Two movie.

He threw himself on to the carousel, between the bears and dragons and serpents that were impaled on the poles, moving slowly up and down as the carousel turned. The mosquito braked and swerved aside at the last moment to avoid a crash. Seth lay beneath a clockwork bear that was snarling and pawing the air, chasing after a frightened deer that was on the next pole along. He listened while the mosquito circled about, looking for its target.

Then it went silent.

Seth pulled himself up. If it had gone quiet, that meant it had landed. That meant it could be anywhere. He searched the carousel for a sign of it, but everything was in motion, the floor rising and falling. The animals and monsters snapped or leaped or ran on the spot. Everything was predator or prey. The predators had fangs and looked fierce; the prey looked scared. At first he'd thought the Menagerie was beautiful, but now he realized he'd been wrong. This carousel, this whole place, had been designed by a mad mind.

His knuckles whitened on the wrench he carried. He wished he had a semi-automatic instead. Or at least a bow. He'd been good with bows. Archery was one of the many activities he'd got involved with over the years, but even though he had quite a talent, he'd given it up in the end. It hadn't been exciting or dangerous enough.

And what about now? Is this dangerous enough for you?

He thought he heard a clicking sound, like a half-dozen tiny feet. To his left? No, over there. It was so hard to tell over the music.

He moved warily towards the source. Better to surprise his enemy than to be surprised. The animals leered and glared as he passed them. His shoulders were so tense that they ached. He knew it was somewhere on the carousel, but where?

There was a whine of wings from behind him.

He spun around to see the mosquito launching off the back of one of the carousel animals, darting through the poles towards him. He didn't have time to think, only to react. He threw himself flat against the side of the carousel as the mosquito aimed for his throat. It missed him by inches, braked in mid-air, and Seth grabbed at it with his left hand as it slowed. Seizing it by the proboscis, he swung it with all his strength into one of the carousel poles.

It thrashed wildly in his grip, but he dropped the wrench, got both hands on it, and swung it again, and again, and *again*. As he did so he let out a yell of frustration, a cry of fear and anger, all focused on this machine that was trying to take his life. He hated Malice, the land that had taken his friend Luke, this awful place that wouldn't even let you escape without taking your memories. Why had he come here? Why did Luke have to die? *Why?*

The mosquito was a limp mess of smashed metal in his hands. He threw it aside in disgust, picked up the wrench again and stepped off the carousel.

"Seth!"

It was Justin. The other two boys were halfway up the spiral stairs, beckoning to him.

"There's more of them!" Justin cried, pointing. Seth looked, and saw a small swarm of glittering shapes rising from the other side of the Menagerie. He raced over to the stairs and ran up them two at a time. Justin and Colm were waiting for him on the upper level, but by that time the swarm were close enough for Seth to see the deep green of their eyes.

"The other little sod went off for reinforcements," Justin said.

"Come on!" Colm cried, pointing. Across the platform was a large building, rising like a glittering hump. One half was chrome, and built into it was an enormous, leering goblin-face which opened and closed its mouth and rolled its eyes. The other part was glass, a half-dome made of dozens of triangular sections. One of the sections, at ground level, was open.

They ran for it, as fast as they could. Colm tossed aside the pipe he was carrying and poured on the speed. The others discarded their weapons as well: there were too many mosquitoes to fight now, and every second counted. Arms pumping, they raced for shelter.

The mosquitoes began to dive.

Seth, always a good runner, overtook the others and got through the doorway first. He was already pushing it closed when Colm slipped in. Justin, wheezing, came last, a moment before Seth shoved the heavy glass flap shut. It locked into place with a loud *click*.

The swarm of mosquitoes slowed hard, and there was a succession of sharp impacts as they landed all over the outside of the half-dome. Seth and the others backed away as the clockwork insects crawled all over the glass, tapping at it with their sharp probosces, searching for a way in.

There was none. The dome was sealed tight.

"Ha!" Justin panted, leaning forward, hands on his thighs. "They're not getting through *there* in a hurry."

But Seth wasn't looking at the mosquitoes any more. He was looking at what was inside the dome with them.

"Uuuh, guys," he said. "You should see this."

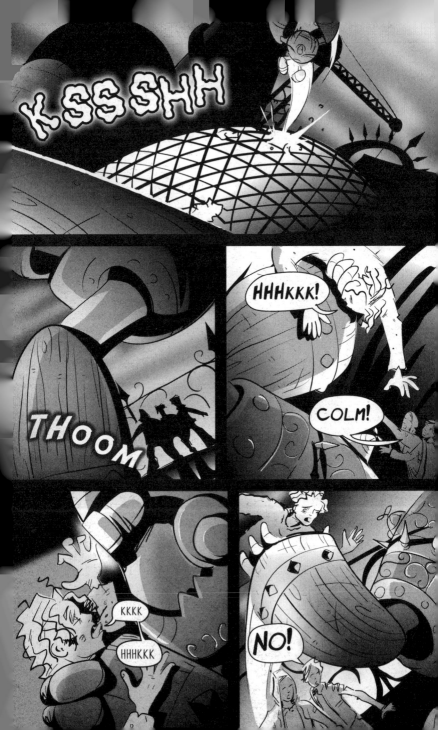

I THINK HE REALLY **TICKED HER OFF.**

COLM'S DEAD.

WHAT?

COLM'S **DEAD.**

I KNOW.

Homeward

1

The last train out of St Pancras heading for Loughborough left at quarter past eleven. Kady barely made it. Someone had thrown themselves under a tube train and snarled up the Circle Line. It happened a lot in London. The commuters on Kady's train muttered about how inconsiderate it was to cause such bother. England liked its suicides quiet and respectable.

Kady didn't relax until the train began to grind out of the station. The entire journey across London she'd been so keyed up that she would have screamed if someone put a hand on her shoulder. Her mind was a whirling mess.

Tall Jake. Miss Benjamin. Icarus Scratch. Grendel. Crouch Hollow. Andersen.

Seth.

If there had been even a shadow of a doubt that Seth's disappearance was an accident or a wind-up, it was gone now. She'd heard Tall Jake's dreadful voice. She'd seen . . . *something* locked in that upstairs room.

And she'd seen Miss Benjamin . . . God help her, she'd seen that woman sniffing like an animal, following her scent towards where she hid in the wardrobe!

She screwed her eyes shut, forcing the image away. She felt like she was on the edge of losing control, of breaking down into a shivering, crying heap. But she couldn't. Because her friend was still in danger.

She looked down at the pack clutched in her lap. In it was a copy of Malice. Probably the latest one. She was afraid of what she might see in there.

She breathed a little easier as the train gathered speed and headed out past Cricklewood. The carriage was empty, the only sound the rhythmic clacking of the tracks. She sat at a table, faced by vacant seats, gently rocked by the motion of the carriage. The bright, flat light made her feel that she was in another world, a drowsy and strange place separated from the night outside. A pellet of light, hurtling through the dark.

She tried to make sense of what she'd learned. Her thoughts were panicky and disordered, like frightened birds, and she tried to catch them as they fluttered around inside her head.

First, Scratch was more than just a shopkeeper. He was the brains behind distribution, the man responsible for getting the comics printed and out to the children who were reading them. But why? What was in it for him?

She stopped herself. *Just concentrate on what you know.*

Second, Tall Jake was *real*. That in itself almost made

her start to shake, but she bit her lip and pushed away the fear. When she was calm, she began again.

Tall Jake was real, and he was working with Scratch to distribute the comics. He wanted more and more children to read them, which presumably meant more would say the chant and get drawn into Tall Jake's sick little world. But again, *why*?

She shook her head. Okay, well, Tall Jake and Scratch were partners. That she knew. And Scratch had some authority over Tall Jake: the man from Malice had submitted to Scratch's decision about keeping the comic secret. They wanted Malice to stay a rumour. A rumour was more powerful.

What did *that* mean? More powerful?

Third thing: Tall Jake had enemies. He'd said so. He'd said they were hidden, or lost, but he had enemies, and it sounded like they were strong enough to cause him concern. That could be useful.

Suddenly she remembered Miss Benjamin screeching at the black tomcat that had saved her back in the house.

"*You're one of hers, aren't you?*"

"*I know your name. Andersen!*"

"*You tell your queen to keep hiding! You tell her that!*"

"This is so crazy," she muttered to herself.

But it wasn't crazy, because it was happening. She didn't understand it all yet, but the glimpse she'd had was enough to convince her there was a bigger picture to be seen. Much bigger. And somehow, after what had happened tonight,

191

the idea that an enemy of Tall Jake might have sent a cat to help her out didn't seem so far-fetched after all.

Anyway, now she had leads. She had the name of a place: Crouch Hollow. That was where Grendel, the artist, lived. If she could find Crouch Hollow, she could find some answers.

She texted her stepdad and arranged for a pickup from the station. The train didn't get in till almost one o'clock. Alana would have gone ballistic, but she would be well asleep by now, and Greg would be okay about it. He went to bed late and didn't get up till past midday, a habit picked up during his former life as a computer nerd, before he'd retired to live off the money from his software. Alana didn't have to know. Greg would keep Kady's secret in return for her silence on the matter of the bacon sandwiches.

The train left London behind and passed into the countryside. Nothing was visible beyond the windows. All Kady saw was herself, reflected. She looked unfamiliar. Oh, the face was the same: small features, California-perfect teeth (but God, how she'd hated those braces), thick, wavy blonde hair in braided pigtails beneath her beanie. But it didn't seem like it belonged to her now. It was as if an identical twin was sitting in another train on the other side of the window, copying her movements expertly.

She looked away. It was starting to freak her out.

Miss Benjamin was sitting opposite her.

2

The shock was like a kick in the chest. Her knuckles whitened as she clutched her backpack in her lap. She couldn't breathe or form a word.

Miss Benjamin could, though. "Good evening," she said. "I haven't had the pleasure."

She was sitting very straight, wearing a black skirt and blazer. Her blonde hair was tied tight in a bun, so tight that it seemed to be pulling the corners of her eyes back. This, combined with her long, pointed nose and chin, made her look like a rat.

"Not a talker, then," said Miss Benjamin, brushing a speck off one of her elbow-length black lace gloves. "That's a very healthy attitude. You could live a long time with that attitude."

"I . . . I don't think we've met," Kady stammered, but it was hopeless trying to pretend. Her terror gave her away.

"That's technically true," replied Miss Benjamin. "But I think you know who I am, don't you?" Her eyes glittered. "So nice to put a face to a scent."

Kady felt ill. "I didn't hear anything," she whispered.

"Really?" said Miss Benjamin, sceptical. "I believe you heard more than is good for you. You must be the girl who came to the shop, hmm? Do you have a name?"

Kady opened her mouth, shut it again. "I'm not telling you my name," she said weakly.

"Very wise," said Miss Benjamin, linking her hands in front of her on the table. "However, I hope this meeting demonstrates that we do not need your name to find you."

Kady swallowed and nodded.

"Now, I have a question. And I expect you to answer it truthfully. That is, if you wish to have any hope at all of reaching the end of your journey tonight." She leaned forward, and her voice dropped. "I will know, girl, if you lie. I can smell it. Don't test me."

Kady's heart was thumping. She wanted to get up and run, but she was paralysed.

"You had a little friend with you tonight," she said. "What's your connection to the Queen of Cats?"

"I don't know *anything* about the Queen of Cats!" Kady cried.

Miss Benjamin studied her for a long time.

"I'm telling the truth," Kady added, her voice small.

"So you are. How interesting, then, that one of her most trusted servants was with you tonight."

"I don't know anything about that," said Kady.

"No," said Miss Benjamin, sitting back. "It appears you don't."

Kady glanced around the carriage, but there was nobody nearby to help. Nobody she could call out to.

"Let us have an understanding, you and I," Miss Benjamin said suddenly. "And I suggest you listen carefully, because I really wouldn't like to have to kill you. That would be . . . inconvenient. We don't like leaving unnecessary traces."

Kady nodded frantically.

"You've become involved in something that is too big for you to handle," Miss Benjamin said. "You've been a little over-curious, you might say. That's alright. Children will be children, and of course you're no doubt beside yourself with concern over your poor friend."

She leaned forward again, and her voice became harder. "You will forget about your friend. You will forget you ever heard the name of Malice. You will forget everything you *think* you heard in that house. This is your only warning. There will not be another. Are we clear?"

Kady averted her eyes. Suddenly Miss Benjamin lunged across the table, seized her jaw in a pinching grip, squeezing her cheeks together.

"*Are we clear?*" she hissed.

Kady nodded, tears gathering in her eyes. Miss Benjamin released her, and she blinked them back.

"Good," said Miss Benjamin, arranging herself again.

Kady looked out of the window, furious at being handled that way, frightened, humiliated.

There she was, Kady's identical twin reflected in the window, her face tight – and opposite her, sitting where Miss Benjamin sat, was something else. Something wearing Miss Benjamin's clothes. Something with hateful eyes, slit horizontally like a goat's.

Something fanged.

Wrinkled.

Inhuman.

She jerked her eyes away with a gasp. She couldn't bear the sight of it another instant. It would drive her mad. Her brain screamed denials at her. It couldn't be, it couldn't be, she *hadn't* seen what she'd thought she saw. She stared fiercely at the table, and started to tremble.

Miss Benjamin raised a quizzical eyebrow, then looked in the window and said "Ah!" She smiled unpleasantly. "Mirrors do so bring out my best side, don't they?"

She got to her feet, bent down and whispered in Kady's ear. "Break our deal, and I'll be coming for you."

Kady shut her eyes. When she opened them again, Miss Benjamin was gone, and the carriage was empty once more.

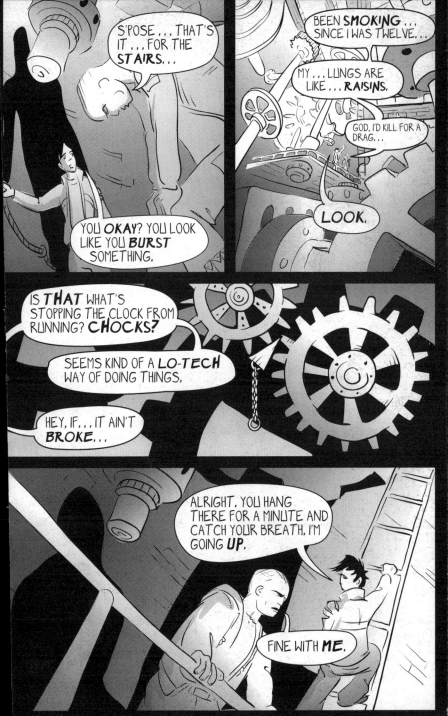

CHOCKS, HUH? WE'LL SEE ABOUT THAT.
- LAY UP TO THIRTY EGGS IN A CLUTCH -
HUH?
- NATURAL HABITAT IS FRESHWATER STREAMS, BUT CAN SOMETIMES BE FOUND IN -
- CAPABLE OF ACCELERATING TO 110 KILOMETRES PER HOUR IN ONLY THREE SECONDS AND SUSTAINING THAT SPEED FOR -
- ARE VERY SOCIAL ANIMALS, LIVING IN PACKS OF UP TO -

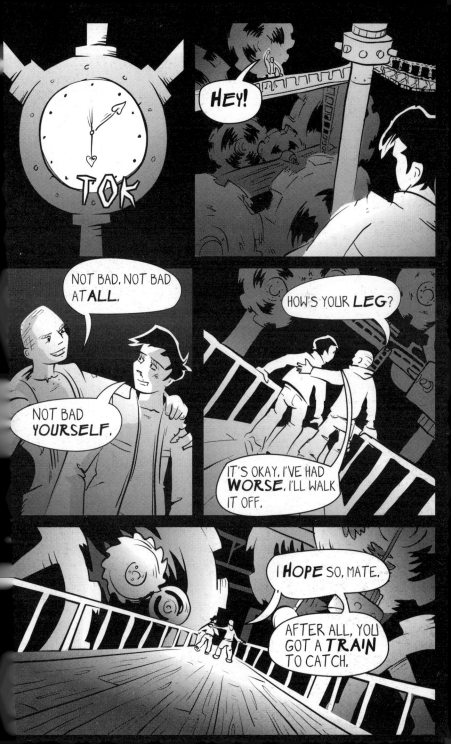

Departures

1

As it turned out, they didn't have to face the Menagerie a second time. Justin had a theory.

"There's a lift, back in the maintenance corridors," he explained, as they searched the floor of the Clock Tower shaft. "The Chitters use it to get down there. But nobody can operate the thing from below: there aren't any controls to call it or send it back up. Stands to reason the controls must be up here."

"Didn't anyone try climbing the lift shaft?" Seth asked.

"Yeah," said Justin grimly, and left it at that. Seth didn't want to know the rest.

They found the lift shortly afterward: a simple set of metal doors set into a stone wall. There was a lever next to the doors. Justin cranked it into the UP position, and they heard the clatter of the mechanism inside and the sound of an approaching lift.

"You can say it: I'm a genius," he declared.

Seth walked in circles while they waited for the lift to

come. The pain in his ankle had faded to an ache, and it would probably swell a little, but it was only a minor sprain. A small price to pay for getting away from the Timekeeper with his life.

He was remarkably calm about it all. If he'd been asked a week ago how he would react when faced with such a monstrosity, he would have guessed panic, if not total insanity. He hadn't known if his mind would cope with something so impossible.

But his mind was doing just fine. He'd adjusted. This was Malice, and the rules were not the same here as they were back home.

"What you smiling at?" Justin asked, and Seth realized he *was* smiling. Because he remembered how he felt when he was fleeing from the Timekeeper. How it felt when they *beat* him. He was wondrously, gloriously alive. More awake and aware than he'd ever been back home.

But he couldn't find the words to explain it to Justin, so he just shook his head and grinned.

"Nutter," said Justin, but he was grinning too.

2

They took the lift down to the maintenance corridors. Seth wanted to go back to tell the others about the Timekeeper, but Justin dragged him towards the train station instead.

"They'll figure it out soon enough. Besides, it don't matter much. It won't be long before something else comes along to take his place. They won't leave the clock untended for long."

"Who's *they*?"

Justin made a vague gesture at the air. "Y'know. *Them*. Whoever decides stuff like that. Anyway, shut up: if the train leaves the station there's no telling how long it'll be before another one comes, so move it."

Whether it was because the Chitters had sensed the demise of their master or simply that luck was on their side, they reached the train station without opposition. The train was still on the platform, an enormous spiked nightmare of black iron and guns. The doors were open along the length of the train, but there was no sign of the eerie Conductor.

"Looks like we're in time," said Justin, looking up at the clock above the archway. It read one minute to seven. "You got your ticket?"

Seth pulled out the white ticket and looked at it. At the sight, something occurred to him. Something so obvious that it made him laugh out loud at his own stupidity. He'd never been much of a planner, but he'd been so swept up in all that was happening that he'd forgotten one very important thing.

"I don't know where I'm going," he said.

Justin frowned. "You're going home, ain't you? White ticket, free pass out of here."

Seth stared hard at the ticket in his hands, his face tight with uncertainty. A white rectangle of a smooth, paper-like material, its edges inscribed in spiky patterns and bearing the number 1 on both sides in black ink. A free pass out of here. With this ticket, he could go home, never to return. He'd beaten Malice. He was one of the survivors, one of the select few kids who had faced Tall Jake's trials and survived.

Like Henry Galesworth.

As he was thinking, he looked out across the darkness of the station. For the first time he wondered if Kady could see him. If she'd been reading about him in Malice, if she was with him as he faced the Timekeeper. Strange, he'd never really thought of it as if he were in a comic. He'd forgotten that he was playing to an audience.

What would Kady do? Was she reading even now, hoping he would come back to her? She could be in trouble. She might need him. Anything could have happened if she'd gone to that shop again. He wished he'd followed Luke's lead and kept her out of it. Now she might be facing terrible danger, and he was on the other side of the pages of a comic book, unable to help.

But even if he did go back, he still ran the risk of blanking his memory. He wasn't *certain* that every kid who escaped turned out like Henry Galesworth, but it felt right. It made sense. That way, Malice kept its secrets. And if so, he'd be worse than useless to her.

There were too many possibilities, too many unknowns. But in the end, there was one thing more than any other that decided him.

I don't want to forget.

He couldn't bear that he might lose a part of his mind

like that. He couldn't bear to forget Luke, or what happened in the Menagerie, or the battle with the Timekeeper. If he went home, he closed the door on a world that promised real adventure and real danger. Not the carefully monitored danger of back home, where you had safety checks and trained overseers and you were never more than a mobile phone call away from rescue. This was life-threatening, wild, a world without rules, a place beyond anything he'd ever imagined.

Would Lewis and Clark have turned back? Would David Livingstone, or Columbus? Of course not. There was only one direction left, and that was onward.

"You're not leaving, are you?" Justin said. It was a statement rather than a question.

Seth shook his head. "I'm not done here. I can't go home." He held out the ticket to Justin. "Here."

Justin's eyes went wide. "You're giving me your ticket?"

"Yeah. White ticket can take you anywhere, inside Malice or out. Even home. Black ticket takes you elsewhere in Malice, right?"

"Well, yeah, but. . ."

"A white ticket's wasted on me. I'm not going home yet. Take it, get out of here. I'll go back to the Menagerie, try and find myself a black one. I bet it's easier now the Timekeeper's—"

"Wait, wait, whoa, you got me wrong," said Justin. He pulled out a black ticket and held it up in front of him. "I had *my* ticket all along."

"You had a ticket this whole time?" Seth cried. "Then. . ." He had too many questions, so he just settled on one. "Then why'd you stay?"

"Didn't have anywhere better to go," Justin replied with a shrug. "Besides, I like mucking around with the Chitters. Fixing stuff. Working 'em out."

"But you gave me the white ticket! You could've just taken it for yourself."

"It would have been wasted on me, too," said Justin. "I'm not leaving either."

They looked at each other for a long time, faces deep with shadows. The train waited silently nearby, looming over them.

Seth was thinking about how this kid had led him into the Menagerie, taken him all the way up to the Timekeeper. He had a ticket all along. He could have left anytime before Seth arrived; he could have waited out the stopping of the clocks and gone afterward. He was a rough sort of boy, and from what Seth had learned, he wasn't the self-sacrificing kind who would help someone just out of the goodness of his heart. So Seth couldn't think of a single reason why Justin had risked his life to take him up the Clock Tower.

"You were really gonna give me that ticket?" Justin asked. There was something like amazement in his voice.

A deafening screech made them both jump out of their skins. It took Seth a moment to work out that it was coming from the train.

"Better get on, mate," said Justin. "It's about to leave."

"But I don't know where I'm going yet!" Seth said.

"Well, what's keeping you in Malice?"

A picture came to his mind: a picture of Luke, his friend Luke, trapped in a basement, devoured by those *things*. "I have to stop Tall Jake," he said. "I have to stop him taking any more kids."

"You know how?"

"No! I have no idea about anything in this place!"

Justin thought for a moment. Seth glanced anxiously at the train. As he did so, he saw something, down at the far end of the platform, hidden by the dark. Twin glimmers of green light, a quick movement, and then it was gone. He opened his mouth to say something, but then Justin said:

"Skarla."

"What?"

"Skarla. She lives at the bottom of the Oubliette. She knows . . . well, they say she knows everything. Lot of people go looking for her. If you can find her, you can ask her one question."

"One question?"

"That's what they say." Justin shrugged. "But I s'pose, if she knows everything, she'll know how to stop Tall Jake."

The train whistle blew again, and steam began to hiss from between the wheels.

"Alright," said Seth, already breaking into a run towards the train. "The Oubliette."

He'd got inside the door before noticing that Justin hadn't followed. He looked back, and Justin gave him a cheery little wave, but even at that distance Seth could see his smile was forced.

"Are you coming or what?" he called.

Justin looked faintly surprised. "You want me to come with you?"

"Yes! You need a formal invite? Get on the train if you're coming! Or have you got somewhere better to go?"

The train whistle sounded a third time, and the doors began to slowly close, folding down from above to plug the doorways. Justin began to sprint.

"Move it!" Seth urged as the door descended, obscuring the view of the platform.

Justin put on a burst of speed, and skidded under the door an instant before it boomed shut.

Seth reached down and helped his friend to his feet. Justin ran a hand over his buzz-cut skull and grinned, breathing hard.

"That was dumb," Seth said.

"You think *that* was dumb? Wait till you hear about the place you just agreed to go to. The Clock Tower was bad. The Oubliette is worse."

Seth was about to frame a reply when a crawling sensation at the nape of his neck made him turn around, and there was the Conductor with his tight uniform, his top hat and that blank white mask of a face.

"Tickets, please," he said.

THE OUBLIETTE

Into The Dark

1

The train came to a stop with a howl of brakes, hissing steam. The doors on its side folded out like wings. Seth and Justin stepped warily on to the platform.

The station was like a dungeon. The walls and floor were built from old, crumbling stone blocks sheened with moisture. The air was damp and cold. Great vaults disappeared into the gloom overhead. Grim statues guarded the entrance: a double set of massive stone doors. Above the entrance was a clock streaked with dirt and lichen. It read two minutes past four.

The Oubliette. It said so on the signs fixed to the pillars. The signs were grown over with mould, but were recognizably the same design as the one Seth had seen in the Clock Tower.

It was dark in the station. The only illumination came from the lights of the train, and from the curious plants that grew around one of the pillars.

"Glowglobes," said Justin, walking over to them. Seth

followed. The pillar was covered in vines, and from the vines bulged large globes that shone with a sharp, pale light from within. Their surfaces were veined and transparent. Seth touched one: it was hard and smooth, like glass.

"These'll be the only light you get in the Oubliette," said Justin. He studied the plants carefully. "Some of these'll last for days. Some last for hours. No way to tell, as far as I know. It's a lottery." He looked over at Seth, and his expression was serious. "You don't want to be down there when the lights go out."

Seth ran his hand over one of them. They were roughly the size of real globes, like the kind they had in geography lessons. Too big to carry more than one each, really. Any more than that and you wouldn't have a chance of dealing with the traps down below.

Justin had warned him about the traps. The traps, and the creatures known as gnawls, and the terrible, terrible dark. And down in the deeps, there were rumours of something even worse. Skarla lived at the bottom of one of the deadliest places in all of Malice.

Well, she would, wouldn't she? Seth thought to himself. *Typical.*

Justin motioned at the globes. "Pick one," he said. "Be lucky."

Seth examined them closely, searching for some clue that would identify one of them as being especially long-lasting. Was that one a little brighter than the rest? Did that mean it would burn out faster? Who knew?

In the end, he gave up and picked one at random. It came free with a soft *pop*. Justin took one for himself.

"It's fragile," he said. "Don't drop it."

Seth looked back at the train. The Conductor was standing in the doorway, watching them. There was no way to return now; the Conductor had taken their tickets. The only road was onward.

The journey had been long. Long enough that they'd both slept, anyway. They'd found a gourd of water and two square blocks of grey biscuit waiting for them when they awoke. The biscuit was hard and tasted like cardboard, but they were ravenously hungry and they weren't in a position to be picky.

"Better than swill, anyway," Justin had said, grinning through a mouthful of biscuit. "Guess it's all part of the service."

While they were eating, the train had suddenly emerged from a tunnel and burst out into the light, racing across a high bridge that crossed a valley at its narrowest edge. For a brief time, Seth had seen the world of Malice spread out beneath a cloudy, sorrowful sky. There was a distant city, a labyrinth and a colossal cemetery. He saw the Clock Tower standing on the side of the valley, and strange birds winging alongside the train.

He sat amazed, looking out of a porthole, and he thought: *There's a world out there.*

Then the train plunged into another tunnel, and it didn't emerge again.

"Is it all like the Clock Tower?" he'd asked Justin. "Is it always that bad, or worse?"

Justin shook his head. "Everywhere's dangerous, but there are places that ain't so bad. Some kids live alright in the City, I reckon. If you can get on with the inhabitants of the Necropolis, well, you'll do okay there. And there's the Marshes, the Barrow, all sorts. It's a big place, mate. You can find your niche if you look."

Seth had wanted to ask Justin where *his* niche was, but he'd sensed that Justin wouldn't answer. Whatever his reasons for helping Seth out, whatever his reasons for coming along, Justin would tell him when he felt like it. Seth was certainly curious, but for now he was just happy to have a companion. He wouldn't have liked to face the Oubliette alone.

"We're burning light here," Justin said, bringing him back to the present.

Seth nodded. "Let's go."

The doors to the entrance looked far too heavy to move, but one of them was ajar, leaving a space big enough to slip through. The statues on either side stood on pedestals, their features heavily worn by time. Seth held up his glowglobe to get a better look.

Whatever these things were, they weren't human. They stood upright, but their knees bent backwards like those of a horse. They had long, narrow faces and only two fingers and a thumb on each hand. It was impossible to see more, for they'd been carved wearing full armour, which encased them totally. The armour was elaborate and close-fitting, and in some places Seth could make out strange and alien designs. They held long pikes with a pair of blades at both ends.

"Don't ask, 'cause I don't know," said Justin, anticipating his question. He walked past Seth and into the Oubliette. Seth stared at the statues for a moment longer and then followed him.

Beyond the doors were a set of stone stairs, wide and uneven, leading down. On either side of them, there was nothing. The light of the glowglobes was swallowed by the dark. Seth had the uneasy feeling that if they fell off, they would fall for ever. A chill breeze blew around them from the station, ruffling Seth's clothes.

"You bothered about heights?" Justin asked over his shoulder as he went down. His voice echoed in the enormous space.

"No," Seth said truthfully. What he didn't say was that the dark scared him more than the unseen drop. It was hungry, eager, waiting for the moment when their lights would die so that it could lunge in and swallow them whole.

Down they went, and they didn't speak any more for a while. The only sound was the tap of their feet and the drip of moisture, and even that seemed to be sucked away by the emptiness.

Seth had begun to doubt that they would even reach the bottom when finally the stairs ended and the light of their glowglobes spilled across a stone floor. They could make out the vague shape of arches in the gloom, and thick pillars carved with unfamiliar symbols. There was no roof to this chamber: the arches held up nothing, and some of them had broken and crumbled, leaving enormous blocks of rubble lying on the floor.

"Pick a direction," Justin said, his glowglobe making his face eerie with shadow.

Seth pointed. They walked.

2

The chamber was immense, and as far as they could tell it was deserted. All was still. The pillars went on in all directions, supporting the arches overhead, but there was no sign of what this place might have been used for. Their shoes stirred up wisps of dust. Within a few minutes, they were lost. Everything looked the same. They couldn't have found their way back to the stairs if they'd wanted to.

Time passed. Their surroundings smothered conversation. Seth felt tiny here, insignificant and lonely. Their feeble circle of fragile light was little comfort against the sheer *size* of the dark. The knowledge that there was no way back frightened him, since he had no idea of the way forward. What if they wandered here for ever, their lights getting dimmer and dimmer until they finally went out?

This wasn't an enemy he could fight against. This wasn't something he could overcome with strength or cunning. He was utterly at the mercy of this place.

Seth felt his breath becoming short. He was starting to panic. His steps became quicker: he wanted to find something, *anything* that would break up this endless sequence of pillars and offer a way to move onward. Time was wasting, and each wasted moment brought them closer to the death of light.

He was cold. His lungs couldn't seem to draw in enough air. Without even realizing it, he'd broken into a run. Justin shouted something at him, but he didn't hear. Swinging his glowglobe this way and that, he searched desperately for a sign on the pillars, racing first in one direction and then the other like a trapped animal.

I won't die like this! I won't die in the dark!

"Hey!"

Justin's voice. He ignored it. What could Justin do? Nobody could help them down here!

"Kady!" he cried into the emptiness. "Kady, can you hear me? Forget about Malice! Forget it! This place will—"

"*Hey!*" said Justin, grabbing his arm hard, jerking him to a halt. Seth almost lost his grip on his glowglobe – it was like it *wanted* to slide out of his hands – but he gathered it up into his chest, hugging it close.

"You nearly made me drop it!" he cried.

"Calm down," said Justin, his own glowglobe tucked precariously beneath one armpit. "Calm down, eh? What's got into you? You scared of the dark or something?"

"I'm scared of *this* dark!" Seth snapped, before he could stop himself. The words sounded foolish. Speaking his fears aloud made him ashamed.

Justin let him go, and took his glowglobe in both hands again. "Listen," he said, his voice firm and slow. "You took on the Timekeeper. Not long before that you saw Colm die. And it wasn't too long before then that you saw what happened to Tatyana. Now you are *shaken up*, mate. And that's okay. There's blokes in the SAS that'd lose their marbles going through what you have."

Seth looked away, nodded reluctantly. The presence of Justin, his stability, was taking the edge off his panic. He began to feel ridiculous.

"It's this place," he muttered.

"That's what it's *supposed* to do," Justin said, looking around. "It gets to you."

"We're lost down here."

"No, we're not," Justin replied. "See those pillars? They're all in straight lines, right? So we follow them until we find a wall. This place can't be *that* big. Then we follow the wall around."

"And what if there's no door in the wall?"

"Then we walk up and down the pillars, row by row. Cover every inch."

"That could take for ever!"

"It might," said Justin. "Or it might only take a few hours. You got to be somewhere? Maybe with that Kady girl you were yelling at?" He grinned.

Seth couldn't help cracking a smile. His fear had faded to a manageable level again, quelled by Justin's confidence. Justin's methodical, step-by-step approach –

a mechanic's way of thinking – had made the unknown seem less intimidating.

"Come on," Justin said, motioning with his head. "This is the way we were going. Let's keep at it. Nice and straight, till we find a wall." He started to walk unhurriedly away. Seth followed.

"You know there's no point trying to communicate with the outside like that, don't you?" he said over his shoulder as they went.

"Why's that?"

"Well, first of all, there's no guarantee that we're even *in* the comic at the moment. I mean, like, we might not be in this issue."

"I don't follow."

"The way Malice works, it's kind of like there's an eye or something. And this eye, it keeps looking at different things. Sometimes you see what's happening to some kid in the Deadhouse, and it looks like he's about to make it out, but then suddenly the comic is showing you some other kid in the Labyrinth who you've never seen before. And you never find out what happened to the Deadhouse kid."

"Seems like a weird way to tell a story."

"That's just it, though. They ain't really stories. They're just glimpses. Like someone's just looking around and drawing what they see. Grendel, I suppose."

"So you're saying that there's no way to know if Grendel is drawing us right now?"

"Exactly. And if he's not drawing us, nobody on the outside sees us."

"But what if he *was*?"

"They censor it."

"What?"

"The words are just gibberish. Whenever they try to talk to anyone on the outside, or give anything really important away about Malice, the words in the speech bubble get scrambled. I saw it happen a couple of times, back when I used to read comics instead of starring in them." He grinned.

"But how do you know they're trying to—"

"It's the only thing that makes sense, ain't it? What other reason would there be? You don't think kids have tried to get people to contact their parents, or to call out for help or pass on messages or something?"

Seth thought about that for a minute. It did help to explain how Malice could have stayed secret for so long.

"It's like religion, right?" Justin went on. "If everyone knew there was a God or whatever, if you could *see* Him, there wouldn't be any question of faith. You'd be stupid not to worship the guy, if you didn't want a good old smiting. But if he's just a *rumour* – and let's face it, that's what He is – then you really have to *believe*. Heart and soul. Otherwise you're wasting your time. The mystery is what gives it its power, you know?"

"You believe in God?" Seth asked, out of curiosity.

Justin made a derisive rasp with his lips.

Seth looked up, past the arches, into the blackness. "Yeah."

3

They found the way out of the chamber soon after that. It was simply a square hole in the floor, from which a narrow set of stairs led downward.

"See?" Justin said chirpily.

Seth glanced around at the endless rows of aisles, fading away at the edge of their little island of light. "Do you reckon we were just incredibly lucky, or is there more than one way down?"

"Mate," said Justin. "I don't care."

Seth was strangely reassured by that.

The stairs took them down a sloping stone shaft, finally ending in a corridor that stretched away an unguessable distance ahead of them. Justin went first, Seth close behind.

"Look out for traps," said Justin.

But Seth had no idea what to look for. For lack of anything else to fix his eyes on, Seth studied the walls and floor, searching for warning signs, but the dank, mould-eaten stone was all the same.

Presently they came to a junction, where two passages on either side went down at a gentle angle. Justin picked the left one, for no special reason. The ceiling was so high that they couldn't see it, but it was only just wide enough for two abreast, so they walked in single file.

"You think this globe is getting dim?" Seth said.

Justin looked back at him. "Dunno. Hard to tell."

Seth shook it. Nothing happened.

"Don't do that," said Justin, resuming his walk.

Seth was looking down at his globe, trying to decide if it really was dimmer than it had been before, when he noticed the long scratch in the floor. It ran down the centre of the passageway, starting shallow and deepening to about an inch.

"Hey, hold up a minute," he said, and just at that moment he heard a loud *click*, and his stomach sank.

Everything decelerated. Justin was turning back to him again, about to ask what was wrong. Seth was running, covering the short distance between them in five steps, his glowglobe falling from his hands. Something was moving in the dark above their heads, something that glittered, descending with deadly grace.

Seth seized Justin and threw him flat against the wall of the passageway an instant before an enormous bladed pendulum cut down the length of the corridor, striking sparks where its edge scraped the shallow groove in the floor. It swung by with a heavy *whoosh* of displaced air, and disappeared up into the darkness again, where it stayed.

Justin had gone white. He'd come within a hair's breadth of being cut in half. Seth looked back at the glowglobe he'd dropped. It had cracked like an egg, and there was no light in it now.

"Thanks," Justin breathed, when he could find a word.

"You're welcome," Seth murmured.

The Slow Walk

1

Deeper and deeper they went, far beneath the ground. All around them was rock and stone, uncountable billions of tons of it. Seth had never been claustrophobic in the usual sense, but he'd never liked being hemmed in. He needed choices. He'd always spent the majority of his time outdoors. Staying in too long made him feel trapped.

The Oubliette offered many routes, but only one direction: onward. Going back was useless. They were stuck inside a maze of narrow, sloping corridors and dank chambers, able to move only where the Oubliette allowed them. The only possibility of escape lay at the bottom, where Skarla was reputed to live.

He wanted badly to see the sky again. Any sky, even the doleful sky of Malice, with its cloudy, pallid light.

Not for the first time, Seth questioned the wisdom of coming to the Oubliette. He wished he'd thought things through, explored the options. There might have been other avenues, other places they could have gone to find out what he needed to know. Was there someone in the City who could help them? A secret in the Labyrinth that might offer them a clue?

What if Justin was wrong? What if they got to the bottom and there was nobody there?

He scattered his doubts. Right or wrong, they were committed. He took a little comfort in that.

Justin walked ahead of him. He'd been quiet for a long time, and he looked white in the wan light of his glowglobe. His brush with death had knocked the wind out of him. Seth didn't want to guess at what he was thinking.

They moved more carefully now, and they'd avoided two more traps that way. One was a deadfall, a tripwire that would have dropped a heap of rocks down on to their heads. The other was a pressure plate like the one Justin had stepped on earlier, the one that had brought down the pendulum. They never found out what it did, but Seth would have bet it wasn't pleasant.

Justin stopped. He put his finger to his lips and beckoned Seth over. Seth joined him. There was a wide streak of foul-smelling slime, pints of it, splattered along the wall and ceiling of the corridor. It was white and stringy, like mucus, and it glistened.

"What is this stuff?" he whispered. "You sneeze or something?"

"Gnawls," Justin muttered, not even cracking a smile. "They cough up this stuff to mark their territory." He turned to Seth, eyes flat. "From now on, walk soft and don't speak. If you see one, stay still. They'll spot you if you move."

That was when he noticed. Justin's face was getting harder to make out. The shadows on the stone blocks had thickened. The corridor had got darker.

A chill spread into him.

The light was failing.

Justin's glowglobe was going out.

2

Neither of them said a word, but Seth could tell that Justin had noticed too. He walked just a little bit quicker, a touch of hurry in his step. A little less care and a little more haste. Traps or no traps, time was running out. The dark was coming, and if it caught them in the Oubliette, it would kill them.

Seth heard the gnawls first. A distant rattling, drifting out of the darkness. He thought about turning back, but he couldn't remember the last time they'd passed a junction, and this tunnel had been heading sharply down for a while now. If they went back, there was no telling how long it would take to find another route. Anyway, he was worried that the glowglobe had dimmed further. It was hard to tell, since the change in light was so gradual.

So they went on, doggedly, towards the sound. At first it was difficult to tell how many there were, but as they neared, Seth realized he could hear dozens. Doubts began to crowd him, but still he didn't say anything. There was nothing to say.

Besides, Justin showed no signs of stopping. Whatever was ahead, they would face it. They didn't have any other choice.

The chamber was enormous in comparison to the corridors they'd been walking through. The ceiling was higher than their light would reach, but overhead there were ledges and broken stubs of bridges, and archways gaped blackly in the walls. A waterway cut the room in half, swirling around the pedestal of some statue which had long disappeared, leaving only a pair of elegant woman's legs broken off at the shins. Great blocks of rubble that had fallen from above lay about like boulders, casting long shadows. The walls and floor were slathered in gluey snot.

And everywhere were the gnawls: draped over the rubble, lazing on ledges, sleeping on the edge of the waterway like pale six-legged crocodiles. The clamour of their tails was deafening.

They were seven feet from head to tail, dull and pasty white in colour, with long bodies and large round sucker pads at the end of each toe. Their tails were covered in overlapping, scaly plates that terminated in a sheaf of rattling spines. Their heads were small and smooth, with blind, bulging white eyes and a huge jaw. Enormous, crooked teeth sprouted from lipless mouths. They reminded Seth of pictures he'd seen of some horrible deep-sea fish.

Bones were scattered all over the room. Mostly they

were the broken remains of small animals, but sometimes there was a bigger bone, a femur or a piece of a clavicle. Lying near the entrance was half a human skull.

On the far side of the waterway, there was an arch. Their way out. If they could get to it.

They stayed hidden in the doorway of the chamber, surveying the room. Seth recalled what Justin had told him about the gnawls while they were on the train. They were totally blind, having no use for sight in the endless dark of the Oubliette. Instead, they tracked by sound and motion, using their sensitive ears combined with an echolocation system similar to that of bats.

Justin reckoned that their rattling tails set up different frequencies which bounced back at different wavelengths, allowing the gnawls to build up a picture of their surroundings in the dark. If you stayed still enough, they would think you were part of the background. He'd read an issue of Malice where some kid blundered on to the idea of standing still, and the rest was his own theory. He always had to work everything out.

It was possible, Justin said, to stay unnoticed as long as you moved very slowly. The other kid, the one in the issue he'd read, had managed to creep past a gnawl that way.

"*How* slowly?" Seth had asked, but Justin had only shrugged.

"Mate, it's kind of difficult to gauge velocity from the panels of a comic."

And now here they were, with who knew how many

gnawls between them and their exit. If Justin's theory was wrong, or if they moved too fast, they would be torn to pieces by a thousand crooked teeth.

Justin looked at the glowglobe in his hands. Deciding if it was worth the risk. Deciding if they should go back and take their chances trying to find another route.

His eyes met Seth's, and there was resignation there: *We have to do it.*

Seth gave only the slightest of nods.

3

The pace was excruciating.

Seth kept his arms by his side and his body very still. He lifted one foot a fraction, moved it forward centimetre by centimetre, then put it down again and gradually transferred his weight on to his sole. Then he would lift the other foot and repeat.

It was simple enough. But then, it was simple enough to walk along a plank without falling off when it was on the ground. It was a different matter if it was two hundred feet in the air. In this place, one wrong move, one loss of balance, one step taken too fast would see him eaten alive. Seth was blinking sweat out of his eyes before he'd taken three steps. His heart was thumping as if he were running at full pelt.

Justin had it worse: he was carrying the glowglobe. Seth had offered, with hand signs, to take it from him, but he wouldn't give it up. He wasn't the type to share a burden. Though it was light, it was difficult to keep it completely still, and though he held it against himself at waist-height, Seth could see his arms getting tired.

Progress was agonizingly slow. Each tiny step took minutes. A little pile of bones became an exasperating obstacle that demanded a detour. The compulsion to hurry was almost unbearable. It was a constant battle to restrain themselves, to keep each step as careful as the last.

The gnawls shifted and yawned. They flicked their tails and rattled. They turned their heads this way and that. And all the time, Justin and Seth were moving further and further into the room, deeper and deeper into danger.

What if they really *could* sense the light? What if they were perfectly aware of the two kids creeping through their den? What if they were just waiting, with a cruel animal patience, until their prey had no chance of escape?

Seth had never been so scared in his life. Ever. This was a level of sustained fear he'd never imagined possible. The kind of fear you could die from.

If I get through this. . . he thought. *If I get through this. . .*

But he couldn't finish. He didn't dare think about afterwards. All that mattered was now.

Focus. Don't rush. Survive.

And in that moment, his mind turned to Kady. Kady, looking down on him as he hung from the edge of a cliff. Kady, perhaps reading Malice even now, *willing* him to make it. Kady, with her blonde pigtails and her attitude, a girl who enlivened the lives of everyone around her. Even when she was being lazy, which she often was, she brightened the room. She was the girl from the outside, who had come from a world far away to England, to Hathern, to give him hope that there was more to life than turning into his parents.

He wanted so much to see her again.

I'm not going to die down here.

One of the gnawls lounging nearby raised its head suddenly. They froze. Seth managed not to turn his head, but looked only with his eyes. Had he moved too fast? Had Justin?

The gnawl scanned side to side with unmistakable suspicion. It held its tail high, clacking together the spines at the end. Other gnawls had picked up on the mood of their companion and were stirring in the shadows. They snapped their jaws and sat up.

Seth held his breath. They were almost halfway there, nearly at the bridge that crossed the waterway. They could hear the splashing of the brackish stream and smell the rank water. There was no way they could sprint to either exit before the gnawls got them, unless these creatures were much slower than they looked.

His back was wet with sweat and his hands were clammy. His lips tasted like salt and his throat was so dry that it demanded he swallow. He didn't. He was afraid that the small movement would bring the gnawls down on him.

Justin's arms were trembling from the weight of the globe. Seth could see it.

Moment followed moment, each one as terrible as the last. But there was no howl of hungry fury, no deadly lunge. The gnawls were restless, sensing that something was amiss, but they hadn't yet located the invaders.

Then Justin began to move again.

Seth wanted to yell at him to stop, wait, be patient. Let them settle down a little more. But Justin couldn't wait. Maybe, like Seth, he felt he couldn't take the fear. Maybe he thought his glowglobe would go out. Whatever he was thinking, Seth had no choice but to follow him. Justin had the light, after all.

They resumed their slow, slow walk. On to the bridge, out over the water, down the other side, avoiding scattered bones on the way. A pair of gnawls were tussling, nipping at each other's flanks. One of them raised itself on its six legs, stretched, and slid into the water to swim off downstream. The presence of Justin and Seth agitated them, even if the creatures didn't understand why.

Some of the gnawls had started moving around. That made things worse. If they came in Seth's direction. . .

Just keep on going.

He fixed his eyes on the archway on the far side. There was the promise of safety. Unless it simply led to somewhere worse.

No. That's how this place kills you. It makes you give up.

He fixed the image of Kady in his mind and buckled down. He didn't know what made her such an effective talisman, but it worked. He couldn't bear thinking of how sad she'd be if he never came back. He couldn't stand to think that she was in danger out there with nobody to protect her.

He caught himself. *He* was worried about *her*? While playing Blind Man's Buff with a room full of bloodthirsty carnivores?

He could picture what she'd say. *Sir Knight*, she'd call him, with that wry twist of her lips. *My hero.*

Okay, hero, he told himself, with a sarcastic inner smirk. *Now try not to die.*

They were on the far side of the bridge and heading for the exit when a gnawl blocked their path. It picked itself up from where it lounged next to a boulder, ambled a few dozen feet, and then collapsed again, right in front of Justin. It was as if it knew exactly where they were, and had decided, with an idle and childish glee, to obstruct them.

Justin stopped for a moment. Then he began to turn to his left. Detouring round the gnawl would take a long while, unless they cut close to it. Seth already knew that Justin intended to do just that. He would walk right past it, only a few feet from the creature's fanged, lipless face. Right in front of those bulbous white eyes.

Step by step. Inch by inch. The sharp smell of the river, the dank stone, the fishy stink of the gnawls. The din of rattling tails and scales. The dim light of Justin's glowglobe, fading with distance, turning the creatures at the edges to shadowed, nightmare lizard-shapes.

As with everything, it was only a matter of time. But for Justin and Seth, time ran out too soon.

They were making their way around the gnawl when a second creature slipped from the water and came towards them, slapping its sucker feet. Seth could hear it coming, but he couldn't turn his head. The first gnawl betrayed no sign that it had noticed.

Whether the newcomer was coming over for a friendly greeting or a fight, Seth never knew. The first gnawl, the one that had lain in their path, waited until the newcomer had approached close enough and then lunged at it. The two six-foot beasts tangled in a hissing, thrashing mass. A tail lashed towards Seth and instinctively he stepped back to avoid being hit in the face. He felt something give beneath his heel, one of the many bones that were strewn on the floor, and there was a loud *crack*.

As one, every gnawl in the room froze and turned their heads towards Seth.

"*Go!*" he yelled.

Justin reacted quickly, bursting into a sprint only a second after Seth did. The gnawls were a little slower off the mark, but once they got moving, they poured out of the shadows, racing to intercept, tails rattling louder than ever.

It was only a few dozen feet to the archway, and there was nothing in between. The gnawls weren't smart enough to try and cut them off: they just came running from the sides, and the boys outpaced them. Seth was in the lead,

Justin behind, as they reached the archway and plunged into a narrow corridor.

After the terror of that room, the terror of pursuit wasn't half so bad. Seth's blood was pumping, his legs working hard, and even though he couldn't see very far in front of him he ran headlong. Justin began falling behind, but Seth barely noticed that the light around him was getting dimmer and dimmer. All he wanted was to get away from the things behind him.

They burst out into a square room, a junction of four ways. Instinct screamed at him before his conscious mind registered the danger. He put on the brakes, but not fast enough. He didn't see the pit in the centre of the room until it was too late.

For a terrible instant, he teetered on the verge of the abyss. Then he fell.

It wasn't far, but it seemed like for ever. A moment of weightlessness, an absence of light, a sensation of sheer, utter terror.

He'd wanted to live his life on a cliff edge. Now he knew what it felt like to fall off.

Then he hit bottom, plunging into a pool of watery sludge. It broke his fall, but the impact still knocked the breath out of him. He was still gasping when the light suddenly brightened, dropping towards him in the hands of a silhouette. Justin. Seth rolled aside just in time to avoid being crushed by his friend. Justin landed in the sludge with a wet smack. Seth finally found his breath, sucked air into his lungs and then threw up what little there was in his stomach.

When he was done, he raised himself on one elbow. The sludge was shallow, only a couple of feet deep. Justin was struggling to sit up, looking up at the circle of darkness above them. The walls of the pit were brass or copper, perfectly smooth. Rotten carcasses of small animals poked from the mire, among clumps of dirt and other foulness. The glowglobe was half-submerged between them, cracks running all over its surface.

Justin turned his head to the side, and his eyes met Seth's. There was nothing in them but emptiness. The glowglobe was failing.

Seth reached out and grabbed his hand, clutched it in a tight grip, a comrade's grip. Two soldiers facing the end. He felt Justin's fingers squeeze his own, hard. Neither of them had any words to say.

They stayed like that as the light dimmed, unstoppably, and

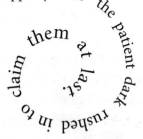

the patient dark rushed in to claim them at last.

Lies

1

Cutlery clicked, drinks were sipped, knives scraped over plates. The smooth jazz playing in the background was supposed to fill up the silence, but it only made things worse. Kady ate mechanically with her eyes on her food, pretending not to notice the glances her parents were exchanging.

Even her mother wasn't talking. When her mother shut up, things were *really* bad.

The dining room was softly lit. The meal was as good as any food could be after everything bad for you had been removed. But Kady didn't taste it. She was thinking of a face reflected in the window of a train carriage. A face out of hell.

Greg cleared his throat. Alana looked up at him, expecting him to speak, urging him with her eyes. He floundered for a moment, but nothing came. He returned to his food.

Kady knew they were concerned, but all this walking

on eggshells was driving her insane. They thought she was worried for Seth. That would explain why their usually vivacious daughter had been so quiet and withdrawn today, right?

They didn't know the half of it.

Kady knew perfectly well where Seth was. He'd gone to an impossible world full of horrors, a world inside a comic. And there were people from that world who had got into this one. She'd heard the voice of Tall Jake. She'd met with a monster hiding in the guise of a stern English woman, who had questioned her about the Queen of Cats.

She'd been given a warning. Stop asking questions about Malice. Forget it.

Otherwise, they would find her.

They would kill her.

Her hands started to shake, hard enough so that her knife rattled against her plate. She put the knife down violently.

"Kady!" Alana exclaimed.

"May I be excused?" she muttered. "I'm not hungry."

"Go on," said Greg, before Alana could say anything. Kady got up and left the room without another word.

She heard them talking in low voices before she was out of earshot. Discussing her, no doubt. Wondering what to do.

Well, you could tell me the truth, she thought bitterly, as she headed up to her room. *That'd be a start.*

She wasn't stupid. She'd noticed that something was

up with them after Luke disappeared. They were jumpy, overprotective. Even when everyone thought Luke had run away, they acted as if he'd been abducted. It wasn't like them at all.

Now that Seth had gone, they wouldn't let her out of the house without an escort. Alana stood at the window after the sun went down, looking out through the curtains. Greg kept inventing excuses to stick his head into her room and check on her.

It wasn't as if they were worried about Kady running away, or being snatched from some secluded country lane. It was as if they feared someone would come and get her.

Kady wished she could use some of the hypnotism tricks she'd picked up from Alana to make her tell the truth, but her mother would never agree to it. You couldn't hypnotize someone if they weren't willing. It wasn't as simple as swinging a watch on a chain and your victim's eyes going swirly. You just couldn't do that.

Alana had cancelled her sessions for the next week or so. Usually she had clients come to the house, and she took them to a small, dim study which served as her office. There, she hypnotized them. They visited her for all kinds of reasons: to stop smoking, to lose weight, to get over a phobia, to access hidden memories or to learn about their past lives (Alana enthusiastically believed in reincarnation). But now, no strangers were allowed in, except the police, when they had to talk to Kady, and even then Alana hovered close by.

Kady had hypnotized Seth once, but it hadn't worked very well. He just got really relaxed and then fell asleep in the middle of Kady's questions. Luke had laughed so hard he nearly broke a rib.

Luke...

She stopped at the door to her bedroom. The thought of the pictures she'd seen in that comic brought tears to her eyes. Luke fleeing in terror. Luke being chased into that rickety old house. Those awful creatures, pouncing on him. It had all been real.

She went in and closed the door behind her. The curtains were drawn, but moonlight shone through the thin fabric. The screensaver on her Mac glowed sharply on her desk. She left the light off and went to her bookshelf, ran her fingers along the spines of the books, then drew out the comic that was hidden between them.

The copy of Malice she'd stolen from the house in Kensington. Still in its wax seal. Unopened.

She took it and sat down heavily on the bed, staring at the red M on the seal. What would she see, if she opened it? Would she see Seth's death, as gruesome and distressing as Luke's? Was Seth in there, calling out to her? Giving her information? Or maybe he wasn't even in there at all. Maybe this issue wasn't about him.

She didn't dare find out.

She threw the comic aside and flung herself flat, biting her lip in frustration. She hated herself for being weak, for being scared. Her best friend was in the deepest trouble and she was too afraid to help him. Ever since that meeting with Miss Benjamin on the train, she'd agonized about what to do. But she hadn't done anything. Every hour that passed was an hour that Seth was trapped in that awful place, and Kady still didn't act.

Why? Because she was scared. Really, profoundly scared.

There was no question now that Malice was dangerous, and that it was more than just a rumour. The question was exactly *how* dangerous. Maybe Miss Benjamin had been lying when she said she could hunt down Kady if she wanted to, but Kady wouldn't have bet on it. The message was clear. Back off, or we'll find you.

This wasn't some bully. This wasn't even a professional killer. This was an abomination.

I'm just a kid! she protested to herself, and was immediately disgusted. Why couldn't she be like Seth? Seth wouldn't have thought twice, if their positions had been reversed. He wouldn't have let anyone scare him off. He'd have gone rushing to her rescue, whatever the consequences.

She thought about that for a moment. She wasn't exaggerating. He really would. He really would have tried to save her, no matter what.

She'd never in her life known anyone as genuine, as simple and honest as Seth. Seth would have done anything for her, if she'd asked. He'd never let her down. How many people could say that about somebody?

Suddenly she missed him so much, it was like a bright needle in her chest.

But I can't. I'm not like him. I'm not that strong.

Her computer chimed, and she looked up. Her Instant Messenger. Jess in San Francisco.

2

<Jezzibel828> u there?

<Kadybug> yo

<Jezzibel828> he come back yet?

<Kadybug> no

<Kadybug> he's not coming back

<Jezzibel828> ?

<Kadybug> he didn't run away

<Kadybug> someone took him away

<Jezzibel828> o no. the cops find something?

<Kadybug> I just know

<Jezzibel828> u ok?

<Jezzibel828> u don't sound ok.

<Kadybug> I'm not ok

<Jezzibel828> o baby, I'm so sorry

<Jezzibel828> this whole thing sux big time

<Kadybug> yeh

<Jezzibel828> your parents say anything?

<Kadybug> like what?

<Jezzibel828> dunno

<Jezzibel828> listen

<Jezzibel828> I need to tell you something
<Jezzibel828> but you'll hate me
<Kadybug> don't be dumb
<Jezzibel828> I mean it. I'm really really sorry.
<Kadybug> ???
<Kadybug> Jess just tell me.
<Kadybug> Is this about when we were in SF?
<Jezzibel828> Kady
<Jezzibel828> You were never in SF.

Kady stared at the screen, dumbfounded, reading and rereading that last line. She simply couldn't formulate a response to that. It was so ridiculous that she couldn't believe Jess had typed it.

She *remembered* being in San Francisco. She remembered buying the ornament on her bookshelf. She remembered Jess finding the white dollar bill that she kept in her drawer. She remembered playing frisbee in Golden Gate, and sitting around the table with Aunt Sadie and Uncle Bill. She remembered a trip to Yosemite where they saw a grizzly, and a birthday party for Jess's sister Maisie. The memories were as clear as day.

<Jezzibel828> u still there?
<Jezzibel828> Kady?
<Kadybug> I'm waiting to hear one real fine reason y u just said that.
<Jezzibel828> I know you don't believe it

<Jezzibel828> but it's true

<Jezzibel828> I haven't seen you since your mom moved to England

<Jezzibel828> you never came to visit last year

<Jezzibel828> I shouldn't be telling u this

<Jezzibel828> my rents will kill me

<Jezzibel828> not to mention yours

<Jezzibel828> hello?

<Kadybug> WTF do u expect me to say?

<Kadybug> y are u saying that?

<Kadybug> I'm very screwed up right now

<Kadybug> I don't need this from u

<Jezzibel828> I'm not trying to screw u up

<Jezzibel828> I luv u, kid

<Jezzibel828> I'm telling u coz u need to know

<Jezzibel828> should've said it after Luke disappeared

<Jezzibel828> but I didn't know if it was the same thing

<Jezzibel828> but now Seth is gone as well

<Jezzibel828> and your parents should've told u

<Kadybug> told me WHAT???

<Jezzibel828> that you never went to SF

<Kadybug> Jess I REMEMBER BEING THERE!!!

<Jezzibel828> no you don't

<Jezzibel828> u just think you do

<Jezzibel828> your mom's a professional hypnotist

Kady felt all the wind go out of her. Her head went light. She sat back in her chair.

It wasn't possible. It wasn't. Her mom would never do that to her. Ever.

You couldn't hypnotize someone unless they were willing.

Had she been *willing*?

No! Don't even start thinking that. Don't even start doubting yourself. Those are your memories. Those things really happened.

But if they hadn't really happened . . . then what *had*?

Slowly, she reached for the keyboard.

<Kadybug> I swear to god if you're messing with me we are friends no more
<Kadybug> you'd better understand that
<Jezzibel828> I promise u
<Jezzibel828> it's the truth
<Jezzibel828> your mom told us what she was gonna do
<Jezzibel828> me and mom and dad
<Jezzibel828> she told us a bunch of things she was going to tell u
<Jezzibel828> like that trip to yosemite, and some other stuff
<Jezzibel828> she said your mind would fill in the rest for u
<Jezzibel828> but we had to pretend that you'd been here and talk to u about what hapepned
<Jezzibel828> she said it was reinforcement or something

\<Jezzibel828\> u might question what happened otherwise

\<Jezzibel828\> jesus I'm crying here

\<Jezzibel828\> I'm so so sorry

\<Jezzibel828\> I didn't know what to do

\<Jezzibel828\> she said it'd be worse if you remembered

\<Jezzibel828\> she wsa doing it for you

\<Jezzibel828\> for your own good

\<Jezzibel828\> I didn't want to ruin it

\<Jezzibel828\> she said u might go crzy again

\<Jezzibel828\> but now . . . I mean, coz of Luke and Seth. . .

\<Jezzibel828\> someone has to tell u

\<Kadybug\> what happened to me?

\<Jezzibel828\> u disappeared

\<Jezzibel828\> u were gone 4 months

Kady let her head fall into her hands. This couldn't be happening. It was easier to believe that Jess was playing a nasty game, or that the person on the other end wasn't Jess at all. But she couldn't, because it *felt* true. No matter how she denied it to herself, her gut was telling her otherwise. Something in her was responding to Jess's words.

She felt sick. The knowledge that her mother had been into her head, implanted those memories . . . it upset reality. What *else* was fake? Could she trust *anything* now?

You knew this all along, a small voice in the back of her head told her.

Was that why she'd been so restless and unsettled ever since ... well, ever since she *thought* she'd been to San Francisco? She'd had that constant feeling that there was somewhere she ought to be, something she should be doing, but she could never put her finger on what.

The screen kept chiming. Jess was still writing, quickly and sloppily, firing sentences at her from the other side of the world. Spilling out the confession she'd been holding in for nearly a year.

<Jezzibel828> nobody knew where u went
<Jezzibel828> after 4 months u just turned up
<Jezzibel828> but when u came bcak u din't remember anything
<Jezzibel828> xcept u had teh most horrible nightmares
<Jezzibel828> like u woke up screaming and stuff
<Jezzibel828> and u were really weird when u were awake
<Jezzibel828> she said (your mom)
<Jezzibel828> so your mom tried to regress u with hypnosis
<Jezzibel828> but u went berserk
<Jezzibel828> in the end she said since u couldn't remember she'd fill in the blanks with nice stuff
<Jezzibel828> so u'd sotp ahving nightmares

"Oh, God," Kady murmured to herself, as the words kept coming. She saw what had happened now. It all made sense. It was just too awful to contemplate.

<Jezzibel828> but then all this weird stuff started going on
<Jezzibel828> like, weird people calling the house
<Jezzibel828> and some guy followed her on the tube once and freaked her out
<Jezzibel828> your mom I mean
<Jezzibel828> and one night she was convinced there was like a wild animal in the yard
<Jezzibel828> like some huge cat or something
<Jezzibel828> they found scratch marks all over the door the next morning
<Jezzibel828> thats when your mom moved u to the country and out of London
<Jezzibel828> u should talk to her

You should talk to her.

Kady looked at the words on the screen. Talk to her mom? Oh, she'd talk to her alright.

But there was one thing she needed to know first. The clincher. Her hands went to the keyboard.

<Kadybug> one question
<Jezzibel828> what?
<Kadybug> when I came back, was I carrying anything?

<Jezzibel828> yeh

<Jezzibel828> I forgot

<Jezzibel828> she made up stories about them too

<Jezzibel828> to explain y u had them

<Jezzibel828> u had like a little white dollar bill or something

<Jezzibel828> and this really weird ornament thing

Kady closed the Instant Messenger, cutting her cousin off. She couldn't take any more. She was too upset and mixed up, angry at Jess for being part of this terrible lie.

She stared at her desktop for a moment, then slowly swivelled around in her office chair. In the dark of the room, lit by the moon and her computer screen, she could see the black rectangle of the comic lying on her bed where she'd thrown it.

She knew where she'd been, those four months when she thought she was in San Francisco. She recognized the symptoms Jess had described. She'd seen them before, in a boy called Henry Galesworth.

She'd been inside Malice.

Kady Gets a Warning

1

Kady snatched up the copy of Malice that lay on her bed. She paced back and forth, staring at the cover in the moonlight. Black. Deep, matt black, holding no answers. Only that bright red six-pointed M inside a hexagon.

She was so angry she could barely think. So scared she could hardly stand still. So *shocked*. . .

How *dare* they screw with her mind? How dare they play out that charade? That wonderful summer in San Francisco, the birthday party, the times she'd shared with Jess . . . all of it had been exposed as false, ripped away from her.

Kady's more rational side knew that they did it with good intentions, but she didn't feel like being rational now. She felt like going crazy. She felt like she could choke on the hate and confusion. She felt like she could burst into tears.

She sat down on the bed, took a few deep breaths. *Think, Kady. Think about it.*

It wasn't just the betrayal. It wasn't even the fact that

those four months of her life – the best four months she'd had in a long time – had been ripped out of her head and smashed to pieces in front of her.

The thing that was killing her was that she'd been inside Malice, for *four months*, and she had no idea what happened there.

Come on, she told herself sternly. *Put it together. Make sense of this.*

She'd been in London when she went missing. Somehow, she'd found out about Malice. She must have gone looking into it or something, must have—

A thought struck her. She snapped on the light, opened the wardrobe and pulled out the copy of the London *Metro* that had contained the article which led her to Henry Galesworth. The article on page six that had been circled with marker pen.

She'd wondered who on earth could possibly have circled it. Now she had her answer.

She did.

She'd been living in London, and she must have heard about Malice and what happened to kids that read it, and that was why she'd circled the article in the *Metro*. But then she went to Malice herself, and when she came back she'd forgotten everything, just like Henry did. Just like all the kids who escaped must have forgotten.

Later, when they moved house, the paper got packed in with all the other stuff. Maybe she'd kept it on purpose, some nagging inner voice warning her that it was important.

Whatever. The fact was that she'd unwittingly left *herself* the clue that brought them to Henry.

She resumed her train of thought. She found out about Malice when living in London. She must have been curious about it. Maybe she found herself a copy. Maybe she just decided to do the ritual. Maybe she even went to that shop?

She remembered something the shopkeeper, Icarus Scratch, had said when she was eavesdropping on them in the house in Kensington.

"Two odious little malcontents came in a few days ago. The girl . . . I just got a feeling from her, something I couldn't place."

"Icarus Scratch, you're becoming paranoid."

But what if Miss Benjamin had been wrong? What if he wasn't paranoid?

What if he'd *recognized* her?

If she *had* been to the shop, it would have been over a year ago. Of course he wouldn't remember her well. She'd probably only come in once. But if she *had* gone to the shop, and if he *did* remember her. . .

Okay, she told herself. *Go with that. You went to the shop, he sold you a copy of Malice. Later you said the chant. Cue four months of blank. Then you turned up at home again, just like Henry did.*

Except that she turned up with an ornament, some kind of octopus-like thing, its tentacles wrapped around a cloudy egg-shaped mineral. That, and a strange play-money dollar bill.

She looked over at the ornament on her bookshelf.

What did I bring back with me?

Downstairs, she heard the clatter of the cat-flap in the back door. Marlowe had bolted in from the garden at speed. As with most cats, he would have sudden bursts of energy followed by long bouts of laziness, rather like Kady herself. She heard Alana exclaiming in surprise as he shot past.

Her parents she would deal with later. Right now, she had something to do.

She picked up the copy of Malice and tore open the seal.

2

Like it or not, she was involved. She'd been involved from the start. Before Luke, before Seth, before any of this began, she'd been caught up in Malice. Whatever Miss Benjamin said, whatever they threatened her with, she was part of this. She'd been to that awful place, she'd survived and come back.

She was angry. At Malice, at Tall Jake, at everyone. She refused to give up those four months of her life. She couldn't live in ignorance, not knowing what she did while in Malice, not knowing what danger she might already be in. They'd come looking for her before, hadn't they? Wasn't that what Jess had said? Then they could come looking again.

She couldn't afford to be afraid any more. She needed answers. And nothing would stop her.

There was a plaintive meow from outside the bedroom door, and she heard Marlowe scratching. She got up to let him in, then sat down on the bed and opened the comic. Marlowe hopped on to the bed and started to buffet her elbow with his head, demanding attention. She stroked him with one hand, not looking at him. He yowled.

"Oh, shut up," she snapped, pushing him away with one hand. "Go bug someone else." She didn't feel in the mood to be nice to anyone, and she had more important things on her mind. He jumped off the bed, offended.

She began to skim through the comic. Her eyes flickered over the panels. It was similar to the last issue she'd read with Seth. Fractured stories of kids fighting to survive in twisted and gruesome places. Stories that started halfway through or finished before the end.

In one, several friends were helping each other through a castle of coloured glass, hiding from hungry ghosts. In another, a group of boys were released into an arena to fight an enormous ogre-like thing. One boy got eaten. She skipped the rest.

She was distracted by a loud clatter, which made her jump. She looked over at her desk and saw that Marlowe had knocked over a pot of pens next to her computer, and was batting them around with his paw.

"What's *up* with you, you stupid moggy?" she asked. He was certainly acting strange. Usually he was very well behaved.

Then she turned the page, and she found Seth. Her

heart leaped. Seth! Alive! He was in the Menagerie with two boys she didn't recognize. They'd just escaped a swarm of clockwork mosquitoes. She read on as they found the mechanical sabretooth and activated it. They fought the gorilla and the Irish boy was killed.

By this time, Kady's pulse was racing and her skin was cold. She knew that what she was reading was more than just a story, and Seth more than just a character. If he died in there, he died for real.

Just like Luke did.

She clamped down hard on that thought, as if it was a dangerous animal that might escape and attack her. She hadn't known Luke for long, less than a year, but she liked him enough for his absence to hurt. She couldn't imagine how Seth felt. No wonder he wanted to go on some crusade to save the world. It was his way of making sense of his friend's death, making it worth something.

Then, on the final page of the comic, she saw Seth's companion take the ticket from the Irish boy's corpse and give it to Seth.

She looked closely at it. A white slip of paper, embroidered around the edges in spiky designs, with a large number 1 in the middle, surrounded by a circle of thorny patterns.

"No way," she muttered to herself in amazement.

She got up, went to her desk and opened the drawer. Marlowe was still busily rolling the pens around the desktop with an attitude of deep concentration. She ignored him and took out the dollar bill. The white play-money dollar bill that she'd brought back from Malice. Except that it wasn't a dollar bill at all. That big 1 in the middle didn't mean one *dollar*. It meant one *passenger*.

She had a train ticket. A ticket to Malice. She'd had it all along.

Marlowe yowled at her. It was a noise louder than she'd ever heard him make.

"*What?*" she cried. She'd had just about enough of that cat. She was about to chase him out of the room when she saw what he'd done. The colour drained from her face.

The cat was sitting on the edge of the desk, staring at her. At his feet, the spilled pens had been crudely arranged to spell out a word.

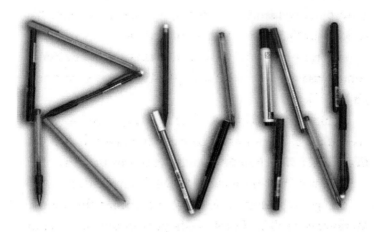

Pursuit

1

Kady stared at her cat in utter disbelief. She looked at the word spelled out in pens on her desk. The cat stared back at her, then cocked his head to the side as if to say: *Well? So I can spell. What of it?*

On another day, Kady might have been too stunned to accept the evidence of her eyes. But today had been a day of impossibilities. Something had altered in her mind. Her common sense had given up protesting and gone to sleep.

Whoever, *whatever* Marlowe really was, the warning was clear enough. RUN.

But run *where*?

Almost immediately she had her answer. Her gaze dropped to the train ticket in her hand.

She stuffed the ticket in her pocket and pulled on her hiking boots, then snatched up a large rucksack from the wardrobe and hurried downstairs. In the pantry she grabbed as much food as she could. A chunk of pumpkin pie (gluten-free), a bunch of organic apples, some cereal bars so dry and hard that she suspected they could outlive humanity. Tins of beans. She filled up several water bottles from the sink and stuffed them in her pack.

What else, what else? What else could she bring that she might need in there? She was aware that every second counted, but there was no way she was going into Malice unprepared. She would take as much survival gear as she could carry. Unlike Seth, Kady believed in preparation. She was always the one who brought along the essential gear on their trips. After many summer nights spent camping out around California with her mom, she knew what she was doing.

Torch. Knife. Fishing line and other tackle. All that was upstairs.

She detoured through the kitchen, where Greg kept spare batteries in a drawer, and loaded up. Then she headed back towards her room, where most of her outdoor gear was stashed.

"Honey?" her mom called from the lounge. She knew that tone. That was the *Let's Talk About Feelings* voice. Alana would sit her down and try to get her to open up about Seth. She'd tell her how she shouldn't bottle it up inside, and all that stuff. Usually her mom was a pretty good friend like that. But now Kady could barely stand the thought of looking at her. Not after what she'd learned today.

She pretended not to hear, and raced up the stairs into her room.

When she got there, Marlowe was in the wardrobe. He was pawing at the canvas bag that contained her climbing gear: rope, cams, quickdraws, a small hammer, and miscellaneous other bits.

"No," she said, as she reached past him to get her Maglite torch. "It's too heavy."

Marlowe yowled and kept pawing. Kady sat back on her haunches, looking at the cat hard. The cat yowled again, insistently.

"You'd better be right," she said, and then hauled out the bag.

She gathered up any other things she thought she might need, including a light waterproof coat, and then jammed everything together into the rucksack and hefted it on to her back. Outside, in the night, the wind was picking up. She heard a long, plaintive cry in the distance; something like the howl of a cat, but deeper, stranger. For some reason, it made her shiver.

Marlowe made a sinister crooning noise in the back of his throat. His fur was standing on end.

"That's one of them, huh?" Kady asked him, though she didn't really expect a response. "Alright, I'm outta here."

Then she looked over at the bookcase, and remembered the ornament. The strange ornament she'd brought back with her from Malice. Whatever it was, she ought to take it with her.

She picked it up. Marlowe leaped up on to the desk, arched his back and hissed at her.

"I should leave it?" she asked. She put the ornament back where it was, and the cat visibly relaxed. "You sure?"

Marlowe meowed and ducked his head in what she could have sworn was a nod. She stared at him hard.

"When I get back, cat, you and me are going to have words," she said, and then hurried out of her bedroom, snapping off the light as she went.

2

She went into her dad's study, which overlooked the street in front of the house. Carefully, she parted the curtains and looked through. Standing under a streetlight, drenched in shadow beneath a wide-brimmed fedora, was a hulking figure, watching the house. Kady didn't need to see his face to know who it was.

Icarus Scratch was here.

Back door.

She rushed down the stairs, through the kitchen, and had her hand on the handle when a voice stopped her.

"Honey?"

It was Alana, who had stepped out of the living room, and was now standing in the doorway of the kitchen. Kady half-turned. The pack on her back condemned her. There was no excuse she could make. She was running away from home.

Alana's eyes brimmed with tears. "Honey?" she said again, and there was such hurt and confusion in that one word that Kady felt herself well up in response.

"I know about San Francisco, Mom," she heard herself say. Alana's hand went to her mouth. "You should've told me."

Then she tore open the door, and ran out into the back garden. Her mother's cry followed after her, but she didn't stop. She raced across the grass, to the row of trees at the end, which concealed a low boundary fence that divided the garden from the fields beyond. She pushed through the trees, climbed the fence and dropped down on the other side.

On the far side of the field was a gate that led to a wooded lane. She already had her route in her head: she and Seth had walked it often. It was a few miles to Loughborough, and to the train station. If she hustled, she would be there before the last train. And then . . . well, one thing at a time.

The grass whispered beneath her shoes. The moon glared down on the land. The pack on her back clanked as her climbing gear knocked together. She didn't know how long she could run with this amount of weight. She only knew that she had to put as much distance between her and the house as possible. It was essential that she lead the pursuers away from her parents. She could lose them in the woods and lanes between here and Loughborough.

Maybe.

Somewhere out in the night, a rising wail drifted into the sky. Something that sounded like a cat but wasn't a cat.

She thought suddenly of the creature she'd glimpsed through the keyhole in the house in Kensington. Was *that* thing out here?

272

At the far end of the field, she looked back at the house. The light was on in her bedroom, and her mother was standing in the window, staring out into the night. Arms crossed anxiously, scanning the fields. Searching for a sign of her.

Oh Mom, she thought. *Turn the light off, you'll see better.* But her mother never was very practical like that.

And suddenly she was seized by a deep sorrow, a dreadful certainty that this would be the last time she ever saw Alana. That she would never again come back to this place and call it home. That her parents would forever think she ran away because of what Jess had told her, instead of the truth: that she ran away because she was tangled up in something they couldn't understand. She would never get to tell them that she loved them, that she was already sorry for leaving this way.

But there was no time for grief or regret. Greg was clambering over the fence and into the field, calling her name. He couldn't see her in the shadows.

She vaulted over the gate, ran into the lane, and the trees swallowed up the sight of her house.

3

The lane ran between two grassy banks, overhung by trees on either side. The cold moonlight was cut into beams that dappled the path she fled along. She wondered if Scratch was already chasing after her, like Greg was, or if he'd guessed where she was going and was trying to cut her off. The cams in her backpack clattered together with every step, making it impossible to travel silently. *Carrying all that climbing gear had better be worth it*, she thought to herself. *But, well, if the* cat *said so. . .*

She couldn't believe how ridiculous that sounded. But the cat had warned her that she had to run. The cat knew what it was doing.

There were too many questions, too many things that needed explaining or answering. Now wasn't the moment.

She clambered up one of the banks and into the trees. Scratch might have been fat, but he looked strong and there was no telling how fast he was. With the pack on her back, she might not be able to outpace him. So her best chance was getting off the trails and into some cover. It might help to muffle the sound she was making, anyway, and she needed to throw Greg off.

Once in the trees, she struck out in the direction of the train station. If she was right, this would be a short cut, taking her straight to the rugby grounds and chopping out a whole section of the journey.

The trees were eerily still. There wasn't a breath of wind, and no animal or bird stirred. The sound of her footfalls, the jingling of her pack, was loud in the small wood. She strained to listen for pursuit. Greg was far behind her now, she had no doubt. But Scratch?

The silence and shadows were starting to freak her out. Now that the adrenaline of her hasty departure was wearing off a little, she began to feel less brave and more scared. The treetops cut out the moonlight, making it hard to see more than a dozen feet around her. And she was slowing down. The rucksack was designed for heavy loads, but still the straps bit uncomfortably into her shoulders. Her thighs were beginning to ache from the strain of running with it on her back.

She hitched her pack to adjust the weight and forged on.

Minutes passed, but how many she couldn't have said. Time was hard to gauge with her blood up and her heart pounding, expecting an attack at any moment. But suddenly she was at the edge of the wood, and there before her was the rugby ground, pale in the moonlight.

It was a small local team, so there were no stands for supporters, only a wide field with two H-shaped goals at either end. On the near side was a small rectangular clubhouse, where the teams changed and everyone went for a drink after the match. Beyond that was another lane. To her right was a steep bank, dense with trees, that rose to meet the road between Hathern and Loughborough. She could hear the distant swoosh of cars, and see the yellow wash of the streetlights.

Light and people and cars. For a moment, she was tempted to rush up there, to the safety of others. But no: it was better to stay unseen. There was no telling how many were looking for her.

She jogged out of the wood and into the open, heading for the shadow of the clubhouse. Her lungs were beginning to burn now. She'd never been as fit as Seth, who seemed to spend his whole life outdoors. All those hours in front of a computer didn't quite provide the same benefits, even if she could whup him at Counter-Strike.

She was halfway to the clubhouse when she heard the cry of the unseen *thing*, so loud that it made her jump. It began as a high-pitched keening and then descended to a low, animal cackle.

It sounded close. Way too close.

She broke into a sprint, gasping, searching frantically for signs of the beast. It had been impossible to tell where the noise had come from. Behind her? In front? Was she even now running towards it?

Something . . . did she see something move over there? Something darting along the hedgerows that fringed the far end of the rugby ground? Something big, big like a *lion*.

Oh my God.

She changed direction and ran full pelt towards the wooded bank and the road beyond, in the opposite direction from the thing she'd glimpsed. At the same moment, she heard a shriek from the far side of the rugby ground, the unmistakable sound of a predator sighting its prey. She didn't look back, just kept her head down and ran as hard and fast as she could.

She slipped into the trees and fought her way up the bank. Branches pushed against her, catching at her pack, scratching her arms. Her legs were trembling with the effort of the climb.

Behind her, she heard the beast crash into the undergrowth. Snarling, it lunged through the trees, eating up the distance between them.

Kady took every ounce of desperation and used it, forcing her legs to drive harder and faster, throwing herself onward. She could see the streetlights of the road now, getting brighter and brighter. But the thing behind was almost on top of her.

She burst out into the open, and on to the sharp downslope to the road. Travelling too fast, she stumbled, tripped, and as she fell she glimpsed a pair of slitted eyes, shining in the shadow of the trees. Then she was tumbling, bouncing, the contents of her pack smashing together. Instinctively, she tried to stop herself, but her momentum was too great. She hit the bottom of the slope and rolled out into the road, into the blinding path of a car.

Brakes screamed. She closed her eyes and screamed with them.

The Last Train Out

1

But the impact didn't come.

Kady had her hand raised defensively in front of her face, as if that could stop a ton of metal from smearing her across the tarmac. But there was no blaze of pain, no quick oblivion. She opened her eyes.

The grille had shuddered to a halt with inches to spare. Headlights dazzled her. The car's engine idled noisily.

She looked back up the slope, up to the treeline where she'd fallen from. There was no sign of the beast.

I'm not dead, she thought, as the door opened and the driver got out. She felt drained, too weak to move. The bruises and scrapes from the tarmac were beginning to make themselves known. *But I'm not dead.*

She shaded her eyes from the glare of the headlights as the driver came round to the front.

"Fancy seeing you here," said Icarus Scratch.

No!

She tried to scramble away, but he was too quick. He

grabbed her by the wrist and hauled her painfully to her feet.

"If I'd have known it was you, you repulsive little gargoyle, I would have been a little slower on the brakes," he said. His small eyes glittered in his pale, doughy face, beneath his hairless eyebrows. His breath smelled of sour milk. "You've led us on a merry little chase. We've been after you a long time."

"I didn't do anything!" she protested. "I forgot all about it, like you told me to!" Which wasn't quite true, but she couldn't see how they'd know any different. She hadn't investigated any further after Miss Benjamin's warning. She hadn't done anything except open up her copy of Malice, which they didn't even know she'd taken.

"Ah, but then I remembered where I'd seen you before," said Scratch. "I remembered you from the comic. You were quite the troublemaker."

"I don't know anything about that! Get off me!" she cried, but his strength was irresistible and he was dragging her round the side of the car, opening the door with one hand.

"We nearly found you in London, but you moved away before we could – how shall we say – *zero in* on you. Delightful phrase. You Americans are so *creative* with the Queen's English."

"Get *off*!" she screamed, and bit down on his hand. He sucked in his breath and then slapped her around the side of the head, hard enough to make stars explode in front of her eyes.

279

"Behave!" he snapped.

Then, the sound of an engine, wheels on gravel. Light drenched them as a car pulled up, and a man got out.

"Leave her alone!"

It was a man in his forties with sandy blond hair, thinning on top. He was wearing glasses, suit trousers and a pinstripe shirt, and he was about a hundred pounds lighter and a foot shorter than Scratch was. But he stood there and he faced down the giant, and slowly repeated his order.

"Leave her alone."

"She's my daughter," said Scratch. "Stay out of this."

"He's lying! Help me! He's—" Kady began, but he wrenched her wrist back and she cried out in pain.

The newcomer had his mobile out. "I'm calling the police," he said, thumbing 999 as he did so.

"Put that down!" Scratch commanded, thrusting one thick finger at him. But he couldn't get at the man without letting go of Kady.

"Hello? Yes, give me the police, please," the man said into his phone.

Scratch gave Kady a poisonous look, a glare of pure hatred, and then threw her aside, up against the grass verge. He slid into his car, which was still running, and hit the accelerator. Kady had the presence of mind to memorize his car's licence plate as he drove away.

"Hi, yes, I'd like to report an attempted kidnapping," the man was saying as he hurried over to Kady. But Kady was shaking her head at him, motioning for him to put the phone down. "Yes, I'll hold." He took the phone away from his ear. "Are you okay?"

"Don't call the police," Kady said.

"But that man just—"

"*Please*," she said.

He studied her for a long moment, then hung up his mobile. "Are you in trouble?"

"I'm in a lot of trouble," she said. "And the police can't help me." She looked back at his car. "Can you take me somewhere?"

"I can take you home," he offered.

"No. The train station. Can you take me to the train station?"

From the trees overlooking the road, a high wail drifted through the air, fading away like the howl of a coyote. The man looked up, alarmed.

"What was that?"

"That's what's after me," Kady said.

He backed away towards his car. "Get in," he told her.

2

The man's name was Graham, and he was on his way back home after a late night at the office. He was rather dull-looking, with a reedy, nasal voice and washed-out green eyes. His car – a BMW – was an executive model. It was neat and smelled new, with black leather seats and glowing electronic displays on the dashboard.

"I have a daughter your age," he said, his eyes on the road. A procession of roadside streetlights *swooshed* by in the night as they approached Loughborough.

When Kady didn't reply, he glanced over at her. "She worries me sick all the time. Not because of what she does; she's a good girl. It's what might happen to her."

Still Kady said nothing. She didn't know what to say. Instead she kept an eye out for Scratch's car.

"Listen . . . whatever this is, don't you think your parents are going to be—"

"Yeah, they will," Kady said. "But these people, they're dangerous. And if Mom and Dad try to get in their way. . ."

"What did a girl like you do to get into so much trouble?"

"I wish I knew," she said. "I can't remember."

Graham looked her over doubtfully. "I can take you to the hospital if you want. There's people there who—"

"I just need to catch the train," said Kady. The moment she had realized that the strange white dollar bill was a train ticket from Malice, she had thought of only one destination. The only other way into Malice that she knew was by calling on Tall Jake. That didn't seem too smart. She had a sense that meeting *him* would be a very bad idea.

That left the train. She had a ticket, so she would get on a train. She wasn't sure why she just knew it was the right thing to do. Something buried deep in her memory told her so.

She looked at her watch. Two minutes to midnight. The last train left at eight past.

"Where are you heading to? After you catch the train, I mean." He paused for a moment, then added, "Look, I'll drive you where you need to go, how's that?"

Kady sobbed suddenly. It even took her by surprise. In the last hour, her life had been turned upside down and she'd nearly died. She was barely holding together. The generosity of this stranger almost made her lose it completely.

"Hey, come on," Graham said. "It's not as bad as all that."

Kady fought down the urge to cry. She couldn't afford to. Not yet.

"Thanks," she said. "Really. Thank you so much. But I just need to get on that train."

Graham's forehead creased with worry. He turned back to the road and pressed down harder on the accelerator.

They drove through the town without speaking further. The streets were quiet and there were few cars about. Kady listened to the engine of the BMW and tried not to think that Greg might still be searching for her, out in the woods where the beast was.

When they reached the short approach road to the station, Kady grabbed Graham's arm and said, "Stop."

He pulled over. Kady craned forward in her seat. The approach road ran past a car park to a small roundabout where taxis waited during the day. Just beyond was the low, rectangular ticket office. A six-foot iron fence separated the two train lines – one for north, one for south – from the car park. A set of ticket gates blocked the way to the train platforms.

Standing at the corner of the ticket office, where she could command a view of the gates, was Miss Benjamin.

Kady swore under her breath. They must have guessed she might come this way.

"She's one of them?" Graham asked.

Kady nodded. She glanced at her watch. Eight past midnight. The train was already late. But she couldn't see how she would be able to get on it with Miss Benjamin standing there.

"You think you can get past her if I distract her?" Graham asked.

Kady turned to him. "You'd do that?"

He sighed. "If you say the police can't help, I believe you. If you say this is the only way, then it's the only way. God knows I can't think what would be so awful that you have to do this thing alone, but I saw that man trying to hurt you, and I heard . . . *something* in those trees." His eyes unfocused as he spoke, and he looked strangely lost. "I'm just a pretty ordinary kind of bloke. Wife and kids. Work in an office. Nothing special about me. But I'm not stupid. I know there's things going on that I have no idea about. Sometimes right under my nose." His gaze sharpened again. "You need to get on that train, right?"

"Right."

"Get in the back, and slip out the passenger side once I've got her talking."

Kady leaned over quickly and kissed him on the cheek.

"What was *that* for?" he asked.

"There is *plenty* special about you," she said. Then she climbed through the seats and into the back, where her pack was lying. She hunkered down in the footwell as she felt the car begin to move forward again.

"Be careful," she said. He didn't answer.

The car came to a stop and Graham got out. She heard the door close and his footsteps heading away. He asked Miss Benjamin something, his voice muffled. Her reply was short and curt. He persisted. She snapped at him. His tone became indignant.

There was a distant rumble. The sound of a train approaching.

Kady cracked open the back passenger door and slid out, keeping the car between her and Miss Benjamin. She pulled out her pack and put it on, careful not to move too fast in case the climbing gear made a noise. Graham and Miss Benjamin were arguing now.

"Look, I just asked you a civil question, there's no need to take that kind of attitude!" he said.

"And what exactly is it about me that makes you think I know the timetable of every train that comes through this station?" she replied tartly. "Do I look like a conductor to you?"

Kady peered over the bonnet. Graham had parked near

the ticket gates, blocking most of the view with his car. Miss Benjamin had her back to Kady, facing Graham, who had positioned himself in order to achieve exactly that. Between the car and the ticket gates were only a few metres of space.

The train was pulling in to the station, slowing to a halt. Kady saw the carriages rolling by through the fence. She was about to make her run when suddenly Miss Benjamin turned around, waving a hand to indicate the train. Kady ducked back into cover.

"There! That's your *last train to London*! Now will you stop bothering me?" she cried.

"I think you'll find that's the northbound platform, ma'am," said Graham. "Unless London is in Scotland now?"

"I know where London is!"

"Ah, then maybe it's compasses that confuse you?"

"Look, what do you *want*?"

She'd turned her back again. Kady knew it by the way her voice had dropped in volume. She peeped out again to be sure.

Just keep her talking, just a little longer.

The train had stopped now, and she heard doors opening and being slammed. There were only seconds before it set off again.

She moved. The jingling gear in her pack meant that she dared not move faster than a quick creep, for fear of making a noise. But the distance was only a few metres. Just a few metres and she would be there...

"If you don't go away and stop bothering me I'll—" Miss Benjamin was saying, when suddenly she stopped. She tilted her head up, and sniffed at the air with her pointed nose.

Then she spun around, and fixed Kady with a terrible gaze.

"*You!*"

3

Kady bolted, vaulting the ticket gates and sprinting on to the platform just as the train whistled. She sped past a shocked platform attendant and several tired passengers, then grabbed at the handle of a door.

It didn't open. The driver had locked the doors for departure.

The train started to move. Kady started to move with it, as Miss Benjamin came leaping over the ticket gates. Desperately, Kady tried the handle again, but the door wouldn't open.

Then she noticed the window set into the door. Many of the older trains that ran north of London didn't have the electronic doors common in the south of England. They still had sliding windows, so people inside could reach through and turn the handle to let themselves out. Kady grabbed the metal lip of the window and pulled it down.

"Hey!" the attendant shouted, seeing what she was doing. "That's dangerous!"

"Stop that girl!" Miss Benjamin screeched.

The train had accelerated to the speed of a fast jog now, and Kady pulled the pack off her back and shoved it through the window with a strength borne out of desperation. No matter what, no matter what, she couldn't be left behind.

"Hey! Don't!" the attendant yelled, for the train was at running speed now. It was almost at the end of the platform, where a barrier prevented passengers from going any further. Miss Benjamin had caught up to Kady and was almost close enough to reach her.

The thought of being touched by the creature that hid behind the face of Miss Benjamin spurred Kady on. She put on a last burst of speed, got one foot on the step and threw her upper body through the open window and into the train carriage. She felt Miss Benjamin's fingertips brush her leg; then she toppled forward and landed in a heap on the floor.

4

Kady struggled to her feet, breathing hard, and stuck her head out of the window to see Miss Benjamin standing at the end of the platform. She was glaring hatefully as the train carried Kady away. Just for a moment, Kady saw in that face a hint of the demonic thing underneath.

She pulled her head back in, shut the window and slumped against the side of the carriage. For a time, she did nothing but listen to the clatter of the train, and let herself be lulled by its rocking.

She hoped Graham was alright. She hoped Miss Benjamin didn't connect him with her. He was just an ordinary guy, by his own admission; the kind of guy that Seth was so afraid of turning into. But that guy had saved her life tonight.

She took the white ticket out of her pocket and stared at it.

"Well," she said to herself. "Now what?"

She got to her feet, picked up her pack and went through the dividing door into the carriage. It was empty except for a young couple who had both fallen asleep. She stood in the aisle, looking down the train, somewhat at a loss. She wasn't sure what was supposed to happen now.

She was still standing there when the train thundered into a tunnel. The lights flickered, sputtered, and went dark for an instant. When they came back up, Kady wasn't on the same train.

She caught her breath. The sleeping couple was gone. The chairs had been replaced by benches of coiled metal. Overhead lights glowed inside cages, and the windows were like the portholes of a ship. The noise was different, the smell was different, the *feel* was different. And yet somehow familiar.

She was in Malice.

"Tickets, please," said a voice behind her.

She turned around slowly, and there was the Conductor. She held out her ticket. He took it from her.

"And where are we going, young miss?" The voice was

clipped and precise, the words carefully measured, issuing from the unmoving hole in his white face.

Kady opened her mouth, but nothing came out. She swallowed and tried again.

"I'm looking for Seth."

It was a long shot. She had no idea where he might be now. Her plan was to head to the Clock Tower and track him from there. She had no reason to think the Conductor even knew who Seth was, but it was worth a try.

The Conductor, however, apparently did.

"He got off at the Oubliette," the Conductor said.

Kady looked into the empty black circles of his eyes. This was it. There was no going back.

"Take me to him."

HEY, I KNOW THAT GUY. THAT'S TALL JAKE.
AND UNLESS I MISS MY GUESS, THAT'S THE QUEEN OF CATS.
WONDER WHO THE OTHERS ARE?
HUH?
RATATATATATA

UUUH. . . YOU ARE **TATYANA** IN THERE, RIGHT?
RRRRR
OKAY. . .
THIS MIGHT BE A LITTLE **WEIRD**, BUT. . .
THAT'S BETTER.
BOY, DO I KNOW **CATS**.
EVEN **CLOCKWORK** ONES.
PURRR PURRR

Killing Time

1

Something stirred in the dark. Seth raised his head wearily.

"You awake?" he croaked.

Justin groaned. "Don't think so. I'm having a nightmare."

"You and me both," Seth murmured.

Justin coughed. There was more shifting, slithering, squelching. Whenever they moved they touched something horrible, something that had become trapped in this pit and drowned in the sludge of water and excrement and other filth that had accumulated down here. The stench was appalling, and even after they'd become accustomed to it, Seth's stomach still roiled uneasily. He doubted he could have kept any food down, even if they'd had any.

They had hunger and thirst to gauge their time in the pit, but nothing else. Neither of them wore a watch and Justin had long ago ditched his mobile, after it ran out of battery.

"Best thing about this place," he'd said with a grin. "No

signal. You might get eaten by a spider the size of a horse, but at least you don't have to sit next to some idiot yakking away on their Nokia about their brill night down the club. It's like these people want to *advertise* how dull their lives are. And the people who have arguments with their boyfriend or whatever while they're sitting on the train! I mean, get some *dignity*!"

He'd made that particular rant not long after they'd fallen down the pit. He'd seemed to be in good spirits even then, even after the gnawls had gone and they'd discovered that climbing out was impossible. The sheer metal sides gave no grip whatsoever. Seth had despaired, but Justin kept up a chirpy patter, chatting about this and that. Eventually, however, even Justin's forced jolliness was crushed by the dark.

They slept sometimes, little snatches of unconsciousness that made them feel even more tired when they woke. Occasionally they talked, but always about things of little importance. Films they'd seen, funny friends they had. But beneath every conversation lay the knowledge that they were killing time. There was no help down here, no hope of escape without light. Soon they would die of thirst.

This wasn't the way Seth had imagined it. After all his dreams of excitement and adventure, to wind up trapped in a pit, waiting to drift into sleep and never wake again.

At least Kady won't see how I went out, he thought. *Not unless Grendel has infrared cameras.*

It was so utterly, colossally dark. He couldn't even tell

if his eyes were open or not. His hair, his clothes and skin were smeared with rank, stinking slurry. Every muscle in his body ached with weariness.

But he wouldn't give up. At least when he died, he could say that he never gave up.

"Hey," he said. It hurt to use his voice. His throat felt like a scouring pad.

"What's up, buttercup?" Justin replied, then laughed briefly and started to cough. "Sorry," he said after the fit had subsided. "Something Mum Number Three used to say."

"Hey, how'd you get here anyway?"

"Same as you. Said the chant, did the thing."

"No, I mean . . . I suppose I mean *why*?"

Justin was silent for a while.

"Fair's fair," Seth said. "I told you my story."

And he had, such as it was. He'd told Justin about Luke and Kady and his parents and his slow childhood in Hathern. He'd spoken about his fears of becoming a boring adult and how he'd tried out all kinds of sports and activities and discarded them all because they didn't excite him enough.

In fact, as they sat there in the dark, he'd told Justin more than he really intended. About how he felt bad about deserting his parents. About how Luke's death just made him angry instead of sad, how it made him want to get back at Tall Jake. And about how he'd had a guilty feeling that he would *prefer* Malice to the real world.

"You still think that?" Justin had asked. "You wouldn't

rather be tucked up with a PlayStation right now, instead of wallowing in this godawful muck?"

Seth had thought about that for a moment, and then said: "Never really liked PlayStations much."

"You don't regret it? Saying the chant, coming to Malice?"

"No," he said. "I just regret falling down this great big hole."

Seth was remembering that conversation when he realized Justin hadn't answered his question yet. In fact, he'd been quiet for a long time.

"You don't have to tell me if you don't—"

"I'm thinking, okay?" Justin snapped. Then he shifted in the dark, settled himself, and began to talk.

2

"You wanna know why I came to Malice, you need the whole thing. Doesn't make any sense otherwise. You, I think you'll get it. Not a lot of people would, but you will, I reckon.

"I grew up in Kilburn. You know where that is? North London, just near West Hampstead but sort of the dump end. West Hampstead's all like upmarket cafés and things; Kilburn's just kind of a heap.

"Anyway, Dad was a mechanic . . . well, still *is* . . . and I got an older brother, Chas, who's got ten years on me. Chas short for Charles, which got him ripped to bits in school, but it was his mum's idea. She wanted him to sound like he had a bit of class. Unfortunately the accent sorta gave him away.

"So my dad was the kind that hit you. I mean, I'm not talking like I'm some kind of abused kid or anything, there's kids who *really* get abused. I just got hit about a bit. That was the way it was. If it wasn't my brother kicking my head in it was my dad slapping me about for doing *some* thing or the other.

"Chas, he was a real problem child. Right off the rails by the time he was thirteen. Dad couldn't control him, and his mum was long gone. Hitting him just made him worse. So he kind of blazed a trail for me. By the time I got to school at five, all the teachers hated me. 'That's Chas Cauldwell's younger brother.' Didn't matter that we were nothing like each other. I was a really quiet kid, y'know? I liked to read all those Richard Scarry books with all the animals. Didn't matter.

"When I got to eight, my bro finally proved everyone right and killed someone. They put him away for ever, which normally means three years or something, but he had an attitude they didn't like so they stamped on him. Fair enough. He was a vicious sod. Hope he dies in there.

"I always wanted to be an inventor. I guess I got that from my dad. I like machines and stuff, I like how they fit together. Machines are fair, right? If they break, it's the fault of the guy who built them, or the guy who didn't check them properly. You're good to a machine, it's good to you. You got a problem, you can fix it. Nice and simple, black and white. I don't get people at all, but I get machines.

"I tried at school, I really did. I had this notion from shows on the telly that if I just applied myself enough then, I dunno, some wonderful inner me would blossom and I'd become this big successful guy. I slogged with the best of 'em. Especially when we got into DT – Design and Technology – and we started making stuff like circuits and things, that was fun.

"But none of it made any difference. Didn't matter how hard I tried, nobody *recognized* that I was trying. After a while you just get sick and tired of swimming upstream. If you're gonna treat me like a criminal anyway, why shouldn't I act like one? Might as well be hung for a sheep as a lamb.

"Me and my mates, we started nicking cars. Just for kicks, really. So one day we boosted a car and I got behind the wheel. Couldn't drive worth anything and God knows I was way too young for a licence, but it didn't stop me trying. I went into a lamp post, hurt myself fairly bad. The others ran and left me when the cops turned up. Moments like that, you know who your mates are.

"I was a kid and it was a first offence and whatever so I should've got off, but with my brother's record they gave me three months in borstal instead. They call 'em Youth Custody Centres now but it's the same thing, basically they lock up kids who aren't old enough for big boys' prison. Wasn't too bad in there, just like school really.

"That's where I heard about Malice. Kids are bored, they talk a lot of rubbish. But rumours about Malice were everywhere. You know, now I think about it, a couple of kids disappeared that year, but we all thought they'd escaped and we reckoned they were heroes. Might be they just decided to call on Tall Jake.

"It's weird, one thing I've learned, you can say the chant and set it all up right and everything, but you never know when or if he's gonna come. Some he never takes ... or at least, he hasn't yet. I think maybe he only takes those kids who really *want* to go, or those who really believe. Something like that. Or maybe he's just waiting till you're all happy, like when everything's going right, and *then* he'll get you.

"Sidetracking. What was I on about? Oh yeah, so there was one kid who swore blind he knew a guy who knew a guy, and he could hook me up with a copy of Malice. I was like, 'Yeah, yeah,' but when I got out I called him. I met this bloke, he said he could sort me out. Very cagey about it. So I left thinking I don't know what, and a few days later the first copy dropped through the door. No stamp, nothing. It just came.

"Things got pretty messed up with Dad after that. My mum left ages back and now Mum Number Three had gone when I was in prison. Dad started to whale the tar out me for every little thing. So I used to eat up those comics. They kept coming through the door and I never caught who delivered them, but I'd sit there and read them till they faded and then wait for the next. I tried photocopying them at the newsagent once, just to be able to *keep* them, but it came out blank. I reckon there's some weird light-reflective thing on the paper that screws with the copier. Clever stuff.

"I used to dream about Malice. I'm serious. I got obsessed. I didn't care what it was like in there. I just cared that it was somewhere else. See what I mean when I said you'd get it? You get it, I can tell. I can't see you, but I can tell.

"Then I got an issue, and most of it was about Havoc. They appeared in the next few issues; they were doing this big raid on one of Tall Jake's stashes, I think. You never exactly found out what, the story kept jumping around like it does. It was just a few guys from Havoc, like some new guys and one lieutenant type who was calling the shots. Dead exciting, anyway. I was really rooting for those guys.

"And I got to thinking: *that's* my thing, right there. Those guys, they don't take any guff like these other kids in Malice, all running around trying not to die. They're stirring things up, sticking it to the man, all that good stuff.

"I think that was the day I decided, the day I read about Havoc. Took me a few more months and a pretty bad beating before I got up the guts to say the words. I really believed by that time. I mean, that's why I was so scared to do it. But in the end I did. You know what happens after, I suppose.

"Hadn't really thought about what to do when I actually

got here. But I found myself in the Clock Tower. After the shock and all that I sorted out what was what, but my problem was finding anyone from Havoc. Nobody had any idea.

"So I sorta dug in. I went into the Menagerie pretty early, got myself a ticket. Then I got interested in the machines, tinkering with the Chitters, all that stuff. I thought about going to see Skarla but I wasn't gonna try and do the Oubliette on my own. I'd read about it, I knew what it was like. Sooner or later someone would come along who knew about Havoc. But then, when you turned up ... I dunno. I just thought, why not? Couldn't stay there for ever, eating swill.

"And now here I am. Sitting up to my chest in stinking gunk, throat dryer than a sandpiper's butt, spilling my guts to some idiot who thinks he can take on Tall Jake and win.

"Still, you gotta laugh, don't you?"

3

Seth didn't say anything for a time after Justin had finished. He sat with his back against the smooth metal wall of the pit, half-submerged in the vile sludge, and stared blindly into the dark.

"You still there?" Justin prompted.

"No, I escaped while you were talking," Seth replied, deadpan.

"Was worried for a moment, y'know ... that I'd bored you to death."

"I was thinking."

"Thinking what?"

"Why'd you come with me?" he asked.

There was a long pause.

"I can't think of anyone I've known, my whole life, who I didn't think would run out on me if it got too tough," Justin said quietly. "Like those kids who legged it when I crashed the car. You ain't like that. I dunno how I know, I just do. That other lot back in the Clock Tower . . . well, except for Tatyana, I liked her . . . I dunno." He went silent again for a few seconds, then added angrily: "Look, I just thought you were alright. You're the first alright person I met in this place except her, and she was all about getting out of here. I wanted to stay. Okay? I just thought you were alright. Happy now?"

"That's why you came into the Menagerie with me? Why you helped me with the Timekeeper?"

There was a few moment's silence, and then Justin said: "This isn't some gay thing, y'know."

Seth burst out laughing. "We're in a pit half a mile underground, with no light, and we're gonna die here. I couldn't care less if you were a vampire drag queen, as long as you talk to me."

That set Justin off, and the two of them laughed until their throats hurt and they felt light-headed. Their laughs became chuckles, and then faded. Seth heard Justin moving around, and then felt a hand patting up his arm until it found his shoulder, where it gripped him hard.

"Seriously," said Justin. "You're a mate."

Seth felt himself suddenly wanting to cry, but it had been so long that he'd forgotten how. "I just. . ." he forced out through gritted teeth. "I just wish . . . y'know. It felt so *short*. I wanted to *explore*. I wanted to go to that city I saw when we were on the train. I wanted to see what was over the mountains. And I never got the chance."

Justin didn't reply, and the silence lasted a long time.

Then Justin asked: "Is it getting *lighter* up there?"

Seth looked up. And yes, yes it *did* seem as if the darkness had pulled back just a little, and they could see the edges of the pit. At first they couldn't believe it, but the light grew, wagging about, waving back and forth, until their eyes teared and they had to look away.

"Down here!" Justin yelled. "Oi! Down here! Help us!"

Seth joined in, shouting for all his lungs were worth, even though his throat was so sore that it was agony. The light got brighter and brighter until they could see the room at the top of the pit, and they could hear footsteps. Finally two silhouettes peered over the pit edge: one human, one not so human. More like a big cat, in fact.

"You two look terrible," said Kady, and threw down a rope.

Descent

1

"Okay, let her down. *Slowly!*"

Kady's voice echoed up the shaft and was consumed by the dark.

"I can't see!" Justin called. "Shine that torch over here, willya?"

The beam of light swung over to fix on them. Justin and Seth were standing on a precarious stone bridge, a rope strung taut between them. At the end of the rope, dangling in the blackness, was Tatyana the clockwork sabretooth. Thirty feet below was Kady, standing on the broken stub of another bridge which had once spanned the enormous shaft but had long since fallen into the abyss.

"Pay out the line through the ATC!" Kady called.

"Through the *what*?"

"Oh, never mind. Just don't drop her."

Justin and Seth began to lower Tatyana. Kady had showed them how to use the belaying devices that secured the rope in case of slippage, but they hadn't needed them yet. This was their fifth descent, and they'd been spared any disasters so far.

"Jesus, Tatyana, you could stand to lose a few pounds!" Justin complained. Tatyana roared indignantly and the shift in weight made them stumble.

"Will you stop antagonizing her?" Seth said through gritted teeth. "She's sensitive."

"I'm just saying, is all."

"Knock it off, you guys. I want her down here in one piece!" Kady called.

In reality, Tatyana was surprisingly light considering that she was made of metal. Justin theorized that the Timekeeper had used some kind of alloy designed to allow her to move fast. The boys' arms ached from lowering her time after time, but had she been made of steel or iron, it would have been impossible.

Kady kept the torch on her and guided her down when she was close enough to reach. Her paws met the surface of the bridge and Justin gave an exclamation of relief from above.

"Well, the good news is, no more bridges," Kady called, shining her torch over the edge. Below her, the shaft continued down without interruption, bottomless. She shone her torch back up to where Seth and Justin were rolling their shoulders to work out the soreness. "The bad news is, no more bridges."

They'd made rapid progress downward over the last few hours, since they came across the shaft. It was vast and square-sided, and crossed by several bridges that terminated in archways leading back into the Oubliette. Using Kady's climbing gear, they'd descended from bridge to bridge, effectively bypassing a large portion of the trap-laden corridors, and avoiding who knew what kinds of dangers within. It had been a frightening time, but they were spurred on by the feeling that they were nearing their goal.

Now, they'd gone as far down the shaft as they could go. The bridge that Kady stood on had crumbled away in the middle, so there was only one direction they could take: through the archway at their end of the bridge.

Justin and Seth waited while Kady untied Tatyana. Once that was done, she trained the light on them and waited as they gathered up the rope and went to the end of the bridge, where it met the wall of the shaft. There, Kady had already secured cams in the cracks in the stone, and left her second rope running through them, giving the boys an easy climb down.

She glanced at her watch. It had been almost twenty-four hours since she'd found them. They'd eaten all the food in her pack and there was scarcely a mouthful of water left – she'd needed most of it to rehydrate them after their ordeal in the pit. Thankfully they'd found a small stone font where Justin and Seth could wash the rancid sludge off, but nobody had dared drink from it. They were all dirty, exhausted, and they didn't smell too great either.

"There can't be much more of this," Kady muttered to herself.

Because if there is, she added silently, *we're not going to make it.*

Tatyana growled softly and padded over to sit next to her. She gazed at the archway, green eyes like lamps in the gloom.

At least they had Tatyana with them, Kady thought. The gnawls kept their distance while she was nearby. At first it had been possible to hear their distant rattles as they kept up a wary pursuit, but after a time they'd given up entirely. It might have been a pain in the neck to lower the sabretooth from bridge to bridge, but she'd more than earned her place. They all owed her their lives.

There had been a kind of unspoken understanding since Kady had rescued Justin and Seth from the pit. After a brief and joyful reunion, they'd all focused on one thing only: getting out. Kady had many things she wanted to say to Seth, but it didn't seem right to say them here. For the moment, they had to concentrate on survival.

Instead, they exchanged stories, recounting their adventures as they travelled. Seth was amazed at what Kady had to tell her, about Miss Benjamin, Icarus Scratch and the Queen of Cats. Kady listened with horror to Seth's account of what he'd been through with the Timekeeper and the gnawls.

The way out of the Oubliette was to get to the bottom. That was what Justin said. He'd read it in an issue of Malice months ago. So that was where they were going: down, to Skarla, to the exit.

She kept the light on Justin and Seth as they descended the rope and stepped off on to the bridge. Seth walked over to her, running his hand through his hair.

"How we doing on batteries?"

"Not many left," she said. She didn't dare think about what would happen when they ran out.

"She's near," he said. "I'm sure of it."

"Yeah," she said, unconvinced.

"Hey!" He put his finger under her chin and tipped her head up so she was looking into his eyes. "Would I lie to you?" He smiled.

She snorted a laugh and batted his hand away.

Seth looked up at where the rope still hung from the wall, next to the archway. "What about that?"

Kady groaned. As with the previous four times, she would have to climb up, remove the cams and retrieve the rope, then climb back down again. As the only experienced climber, she wouldn't let anyone else do it.

"I'm too tired," she said. "Let's just rest for a bit. I'll do it after."

Seth gave her a concerned look. She waved him away.

"I'm fine, Seth, I'm just . . . I dunno. Doesn't this place ever end?"

"We're right there, Kady. Don't give up."

She shone her Maglite at him. "You know, your never-say-die attitude can really get on a girl's nerves," she said wearily.

2

They rested for a time and drank the last of the water, then Kady went up and reclaimed her climbing gear from the wall. Seth shrugged on the pack. He'd carried it for her ever since the pit, and Kady was happy to let him.

Beyond the archway was a cavernous corridor with a high, mould-speckled ceiling. It was built differently to the dungeon-like rooms they were used to. Here, it was possible to see faded patterns and bits of murals, hinting that this place was once grand. The walls were not built of huge stone blocks but were smooth instead. Kady's torch beam found the arm of a statue lying on the floor, though its owner was nowhere to be seen.

They might have stopped to investigate further, but they were too excited by what was at the end of the corridor. There, they saw a hexagonal portal, and a pale green glow came from the room beyond.

"It's about time," Justin said, and set off towards it. But Kady grabbed his arm.

"Wait," she said. She sniffed the air.

Now the others noticed it too. Rot and decay. A musty, stale reek: the smell of old deaths.

"Careful," she murmured, releasing him.

"Right," Justin said.

The place beyond the portal was wonderful and terrible all at once.

It was cold, colder than the damp chill of the Oubliette, and the air was full of whispers. Their breath steamed the air as they stepped inside, and stared at what they'd found.

It had the feeling of a sacred place, a temple or church, but it had been horribly defiled. Spiralling pillars of what looked like black and purple glass rose up from the smooth floor, but most of them were broken and lay in pieces. Elaborate alcoves had once sheltered statues; all had been tipped and smashed.

The only part of the chamber that seemed undamaged was in the centre of the room. It was a life-size statue of a woman holding an ornate bow. She was standing on a hexagonal pedestal with the bow tilted upwards towards the ceiling, as if aiming at something overhead. At the foot of the pedestal was an altar, a huge slab of black glass. Growing from its centre was a small, petrified tree, dead and white. Silver chimes dangled from its branches.

The eerie glow was coming from the walls and floor, and it fell on the bodies strewn at the foot of the pedestal, and scattered between the pillars. There were several dozen, long dead, and most certainly not human.

"Oh, wow," Kady said. "Look."

They followed her gaze upwards. The roof of the chamber couldn't be seen. Instead, it was claimed by darkness, and speckled with stars. There were bright nebulae up there, colourful clouds of interstellar gas, distant galaxies and star nurseries. It was a universe, impossibly far and yet close enough that it seemed they could have climbed one of the unbroken pillars and brushed it with outstretched fingers.

"What *is* this place?" Seth murmured.

"I think it's a shrine," said Kady. "I mean, it *was*. Now, I don't know."

"A shrine to *what*, though?"

Justin thumbed at the statue. "To her, I reckon."

Seth slid the pack off his back and laid it against a wall, then walked over to crouch next to one of the bodies. There was little left of them now, except for bones and armour. The smell of decay was unpleasant but not overpowering.

"I recognize these guys," Kady said.

"From the gateway to the Oubliette," Seth said, nodding. "There were two statues."

And now here were the models, or their skeletons at least. Their armour was of a blue-black metal, engraved with swirling designs. It was made to encase long, narrow skulls, thin bodies, powerful legs with reversed knees. Most carried double-bladed pikes, but some had elaborate bows, and wore quivers on their backs. Seth wondered what they looked like when they were alive.

"You hear that?" Justin asked, cocking his head. He'd wandered over to the statue and was studying it. "Don't it sound like people talking?"

Kady walked over to him, picking her way through the bodies. She *could* hear it, the soft and constant whispering, as of many voices. It was too faint to make out words, but it didn't sound like English. It made her skin crawl.

But there was something else unsettling her, too. A nagging memory: something she couldn't quite recall.

"You think they all killed each other?" Justin asked.

"Don't think so," said Seth. "Some of these guys got crushed. They weren't killed by blades, they were killed by something big." He scratched the back of his neck. "I get the feeling they were defending this place. I mean, there's statues of them at the entrance, right? Maybe they're like guardians."

"Maybe," said Justin, noncommittal.

Kady examined the statue. There wasn't so much as a scratch on it. It was carved from something like obsidian, but it reflected nothing. Utterly black, it seemed to suck the light and heat out of the room. Standing next to it was like standing in front of a freezer with the door open.

The bow was made of something different. It was of a dark, dark wood, its surface chased with thorny designs. Though it was held at full draw by the statue, it wasn't part of the statue itself. Kady suspected it had been placed in the statue's hands after it was carved.

The woman herself was extraordinarily beautiful, wearing a cloak and elegant hunting gear. Her face was tilted to the galaxies above, and her expression was stern.

There's stars . . . stars underground.

A voice. Desperate, frightened, sounding in her memory. And suddenly she knew who it was. Henry Galesworth, the boy she'd hypnotized. The boy who'd escaped from Malice.

The lady wants to shoot out the stars!

Kady put her hand to her mouth. Henry Galesworth had been here. He'd been in the Oubliette, and he'd survived.

She racked her brains: what else did he say? Something about the dark, something about how his brother got eaten – eaten by gnawls, no doubt. He said to follow the eyes, though who knew what *that* meant. And what else, what else?

Justin was peering closely at the chimes hanging from the petrified tree on the altar. They were transparent, fragile as icicles. He poked one of them experimentally.

The bells bring the beast. That was what Henry said. *The bells bring the beast.*

"*Don't touch them!*" Kady cried, but she was an instant too late. Justin flicked one of the chimes with his fingernail. A high, pure tone sang out.

"Why not?" Justin frowned, shrugging as he stepped back.

But the tone didn't fade. Instead, it was joined by others, higher and lower in pitch, the voices of different chimes. They grew in volume, rising and rising, combining into one monstrous chord, echoing from the walls and making the glass pillars tremble. Tatyana cringed and the others covered their ears as the sound became deafening . . . and then, at once, it stopped, ringing away into silence.

The whispers had ceased. Everything was still.

From an arch on the far side of the chamber, they heard a low, gurgling roar. The sound of something huge. The sound of the beast approaching.

"*That's* why not," Kady said.

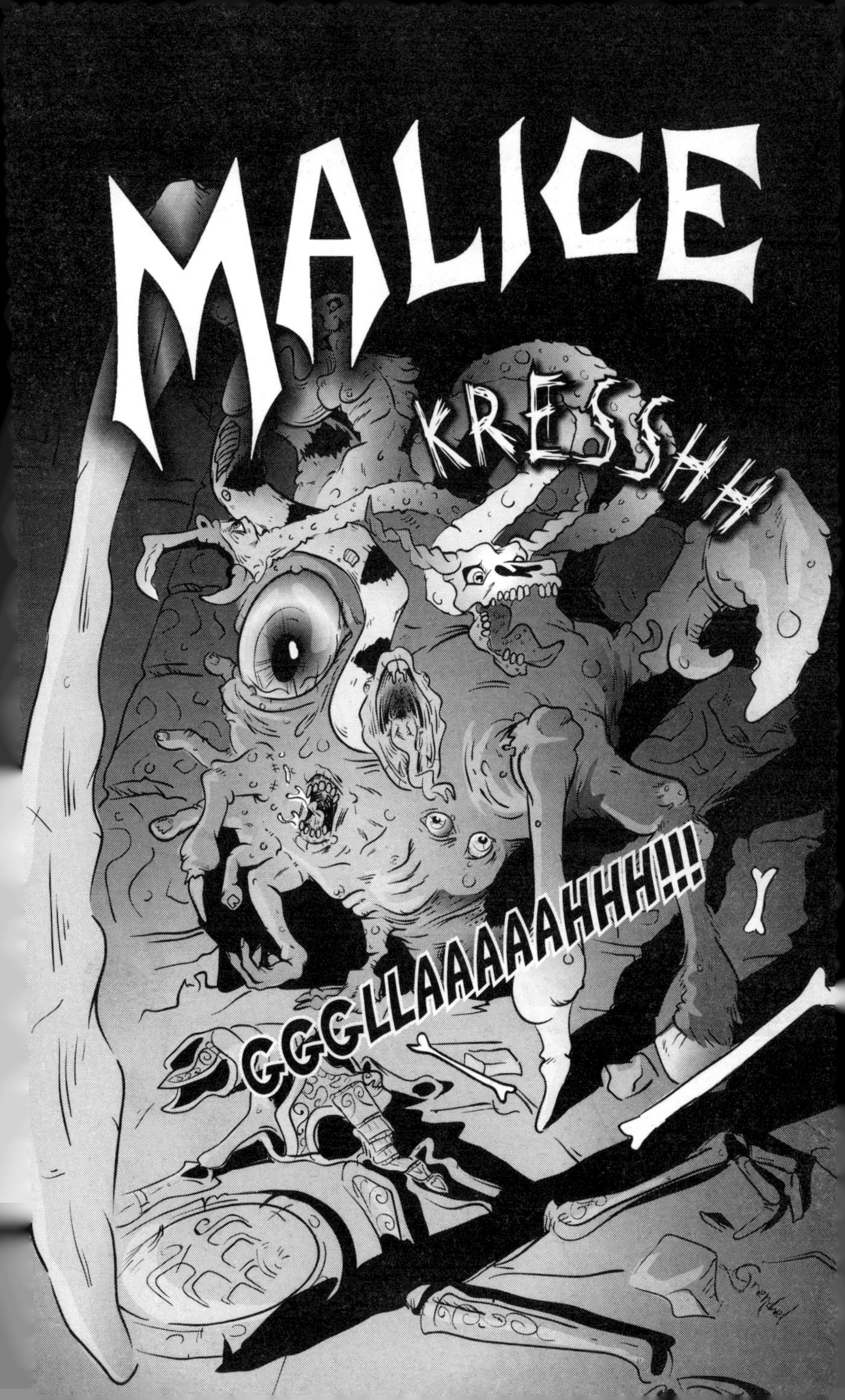
MALICE
KRESSHH
GGGLLAAAAAAHHH!!!

KADY, I CAN'T **SEE**.

WE'RE GONNA BREAK OUR **NECKS** LIKE THIS.

WAIT A MINUTE, I JUST NEED TO –

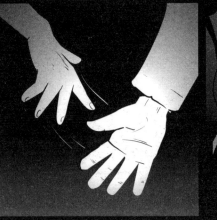

KRAAAAH!

SKAIIIEEEE!

OKAY, SETH.

YOU GOT YOURSELF **INTO** THIS.

THINK.

YEAH.

I HAVE NEED OF A CHAMPION.

I CHOOSE YOU.

Eyes

1

"Seth! Seth!"

His eyes flew open and he screamed. For a few moments, he didn't understand where he was. His head was filled with the freezing, sucking void; empty, eternal and eternally without hope. He was cold, so very cold, and he was shivering violently, teeth chattering.

Then he focused on Kady, who was kneeling in front of him, shaking him where he lay. She was dirty and tired and her hair was tangled, but here was *life*. He reached out his arms and clung to her, pressing himself against her warmth. It was only then that he saw the frost on his clothes, and noticed that his fingers had gone blue.

"Here," said Justin, holding out his hoodie. "Put this on him."

Kady helped Seth's arms through the sleeves of the hoodie, and pulled up the hood over his head. Then she hugged herself to him again.

"Come on," she said to Justin. "Come here and hug him. He needs the body heat."

"It ain't *that* desperate," Justin said uneasily. "Look, he's already getting some colour back."

And he was. His shivers receded to occasional bursts of trembling. His fingers prickled with pins and needles as blood warmed them again. His teeth stopped chattering.

"Tatyana. . ." he muttered. "Is she. . ."

"She's fine," said Justin, and Seth felt his shoulder butted by a metal muzzle. He turned his head and managed a smile at the sight of the clockwork sabretooth. She butted him again, hard enough to shunt him a few inches along the floor. Her way of a thank you, he guessed. Whatever else had come out of it, he'd certainly scored points with the cat.

"You're okay, aren't you?" he said. "Takes more than being thrown through a pillar to put you down, eh?" Tatyana began to purr, a deep rumble with a faint undertone of clanking.

"Just you worry about yourself," Justin said. "You look like you just wandered out of a meat locker."

"What happened to you?" Kady asked.

Seth sat up with some effort and saw the bow lying a few feet away from him. There was no trace of the strange energy it had blazed with moments before. He stared at the statue of the huntswoman on the pedestal, standing there without her weapon, her arm still drawn back as if to shoot out the stars overhead.

He remembered a voice. A woman's voice, chilly as the grave.

"I don't know what happened," he muttered. "I don't know."

2

Seth recovered quickly. He was weary, and his body ached, but once he'd warmed up, he felt himself again. Kady had gone to explore up the corridor with Justin, leaving Tatyana to guard him. He sat against a pillar and rested.

I have need of a champion, the voice had said. *I choose you.*

What did *that* mean?

He looked at where the bow lay. Nobody had dared touch it since it had fallen from his hands, but it drew his gaze. He couldn't help it. It was beautiful: a recurve longbow made of the blackest wood he'd ever seen. It shone faintly, reflecting the pale green glow of the shrine.

It belonged to the woman on the pedestal, the woman this place had been built to worship. She'd *touched* him somehow. He felt changed, but he couldn't understand how. All he knew was that the voice he heard must have been hers: the mysterious huntswoman. In slaying the Mort-Beast, he'd unwittingly removed the intruder that had destroyed her shrine and killed her followers. He was only trying to save Tatyana, but...

What had he done?

He wondered briefly if he should take the bow with him, but he decided against it. The bow belonged to the lady. He'd no right to take it from this place. Instead, he picked himself up and walked slowly over to it.

He didn't want to touch it. Lurking on the edge of his mind was the memory of that terrible, all-swallowing abyss. But the sight of the statue without the bow in its hands troubled him. It felt somehow disrespectful to leave without putting back what he'd borrowed.

His hand closed around the bow. No strange energy lashed him this time, no freezing touch. The wood was cold, but no more.

He brought it over to the statue. The woman stood where she'd always stood, leaching the eerie light from the room, but now there seemed a new majesty about her. Seth couldn't say why – nothing had physically changed – but she seemed *grander* somehow.

With a little difficulty, he got the bow back into her hands. As an afterthought, he picked an arrow from the quiver of a dead guardian and set it in place. When he stepped back and looked, the statue was just as it had been when they entered, with the lady aiming her arrow at the galaxies above.

Who is she? he thought.

At that moment, he heard running footsteps. Kady and Justin emerged from the archway, beaming excitedly.

"You won't believe this," Justin said. "But I reckon she found the way to Skarla's place."

3

"See, when we first got to the temple, I remembered about Henry Galesworth," Kady said. "Not fast enough to stop Genius here from striking the chimes, though."

"Hey!" said Justin. "You show me anyone who *wouldn't*

tap a set of chimes just to see what they sound like."

They were standing in the dark of the corridor. The green light of the temple was some way behind them. Kady's torch was the only illumination now.

"Anyway, so after I figured out everything else that Henry had said, there was one thing left that didn't add up. *Follow the eyes*, he said." She grinned. "Check it out."

She shone her torch at the wall, where a crude eye had been daubed with flaky red paint. Next to it was a narrow corridor leading off from the main one.

Kady bowed to each of them. "Thank you, thank you. Hold the applause. No, really, you're too kind."

"Nice one, Kady," Seth said.

"I am great, though, aren't I?"

"Modest, too," Justin put in.

"You noticed that?"

Seth studied the eye. "How on earth that porky, blubbering kid got through this place alive I'll never know," he mused.

"Maybe he was different back then," Kady suggested. "Maybe he only ended up like that because of what happened to him."

"Am I the only one who cares that we have only one torch and very few batteries left?" Justin said. "Can we get going? If this kid said follow the eyes, let's follow the eyes."

They followed the eyes. Through thin, winding corridors, along sloping passageways, down a long flight of spiral stairs. At each turn, an eye was smeared on the wall in the same red paint.

It was an hour later by Kady's watch that they found what they were looking for.

Skarla

1

At the end of a long stone corridor was a door. It was small, made of wood, and all around it was a tangle of roots that had broken through the stone blocks of the corridor and crawled over the floor and ceiling. Small mushrooms and moulds huddled in the folds of the roots, and strange black flowers grew down here, even without any light.

"Feels like for ever since I saw anything that grows," Seth muttered. "This place is so dead."

"Do we knock?" Kady asked, then answered her own question. "Let's knock."

Seth looked at Justin, who shrugged. "S'pose so. I don't know anything more about this place than I already told you. Her name's Skarla. She's like a wise woman or something. She'll answer your questions. And then she'll show us the way out of this place. That's the rumour, anyway."

"It better be more than a rumour," Kady said as she rapped on the door.

They waited. After a time they heard movement.

"I just *know* she's gonna be weird-looking," Kady muttered.

The door opened, and soft light flooded out and across their faces. Firelight. Welcoming, warming light, promising safety. After days in this hellish dungeon, Seth thought he'd never seen anything so beautiful.

Standing in the doorway was Skarla. And Kady hadn't been wrong.

She was only about five feet tall, though she walked with a stoop. She wore a cowled brown cloak and a coarse robe beneath it of the same colour. Much of her was covered, except her hands and face. But those were enough to see that she wasn't even close to human.

More than anything, she seemed to be a plant. Her hands were a cluster of earthy brown roots. What they could see of her face was little more than a long, walrus-like cluster of dirt-caked tendrils that hid her mouth, and a pair of large amber eyes.

It was the eyes that set them at ease. They were kind, lashed with grass, and somehow they conveyed that she was female. Even in such a strange creature, the eyes were the windows to the soul. In hers, they saw only grandmotherly affection.

"Well, don't just stand out there," she said, her voice dry and cracked. "You've come a long way to see me, haven't you?"

She turned and shuffled back into the room. They stepped inside and shut the door behind them.

Skarla's home was cramped and cluttered, and smelled of soil: a fresh, clean smell after the dank reek of the Oubliette. The ceiling was low and everywhere were shelves of dusty jars, bizarre apparatuses, sheaves of herbs hanging from racks. The walls were packed earth, and the rooms were unevenly

347

shaped. In one was a small pool of water, surrounded by coloured stones, that they had to step around.

The place had the feel of a magician's cave, stuffed with odd and fascinating objects that occupied every nook. There were tin figurines, petrified claws, tiny jewelled boxes, feathers, spooky dolls, and in one case a small bag of teeth. Lamps shone with a friendly glow.

They followed her through several chambers to where a fire burned in a hearth. Here was another, larger pool, also surrounded by stones of many colours and types. There were two battered armchairs against one wall, and an alcove into which crude shelves had been set. Next to it was a small, round wooden door, which was closed. At the far end was a large glass globe cradled in a pedestal of roots that seemed to have grown out of the ground.

"Sit down, sit down," she creaked. She shuffled over to the pool and stepped into it, groaning with relief, as if the journey through the house had worn her out. When they hesitated, she waved at them. "The chairs are for visitors. I don't use them. I'm afraid there aren't enough for all of you. I don't usually get such big groups."

She settled herself into a hunch. Kady sat down, and after a moment Justin did too. Seth remained standing. Tatyana slunk into the room, examined it critically, then flopped down in front of the fire and fell asleep.

"I'm sorry I can't offer you refreshments," she said. "But I don't think there's anything here you'd like."

"That's okay," said Seth. "If you don't mind, we'd like

to ask you our questions and get on as quick as possible. I think we've all had enough of the Oubliette."

"Of course," Skarla said, and her whiskery tendrils moved in what might have been a smile. "Let's get some things straight, though, because my reputation has gotten a little out of hand lately. No, I *don't* know everything. But I do know a lot. Yes, I can send you back home, if that's what you want. And you get *one* question."

"Each?" Kady asked, then clapped her hand over her mouth. "That wasn't the question!" she blurted.

"Don't worry, child. I'm not like that. You may ask as many *little* questions as you wish, but you have one *big* question between you, so think carefully before you ask. The process is very tiring, and I'm not the shoot I once was."

"What's the difference?" Justin asked, before quickly adding, "That was a little question, right?" He thought for a moment, then said, "So was that."

Skarla cackled in delight. "You're sweet, child," she said. "A little question is one I can easily answer. A big one is a question I have to *seek*. I won't trick you."

Seth looked at the others. "Well, I know what I want to ask."

Kady waved at him. "Fine with me. I've got a million questions, but they all end up at the same thing. How do we stop Tall Jake?"

"That ain't *my* question," Justin said.

Kady sighed. "What's yours?"

"I want to know how to find Havoc."

She frowned. "Why do I know that name? Oh, right, I remember. Back in the house in Kensington. Scratch and Miss Benjamin were talking about it."

"I want to find 'em. I want to *join* 'em."

"What about all the kids who are getting taken by Tall Jake?" said Seth.

"He's ain't taking *anyone* that doesn't ask," Justin pointed out. "I knew what I was doing when I came here. I reckon you did, too. There's others like us, who think that taking the risk of coming here is better than what we've got there. If the average muppet is too daft to look before they leap, why's that our problem?"

"Because kids are *dying* here!" Seth cried.

"Kids are dying everywhere," Justin said. "Anyway, Havoc are fighting *against* Tall Jake," Justin said. "If we find them, well, maybe we can kill two birds with one stone."

"But what if they don't know how to win? Skarla can tell us how to *stop* him," Seth said, then turned to her. "Can't you?"

"Perhaps," she said, the fire glinting in her amber eyes.

Seth thought for a moment. One question. Justin was right, it was possible that Havoc already knew how to stop all this. But it was also possible they had no idea. They might be fighting a futile guerrilla war against a hopeless enemy.

And there were so many other things to ask. What did Tall Jake want? What did Scratch have to do with it? What was their plan? What *was* the world of Malice? How could it even exist?

But to him, there was only one thing that was important. He'd seen what happened to Luke. He'd seen how Luke's disappearance destroyed his mother. Whatever Justin thought, Malice was tearing people's lives apart. If they took out Tall Jake, maybe they could stop that.

He wandered over to the far end of the room, where the glass globe was cupped inside a mass of knotted roots. He heard the gentle splashing of water, and Skarla came over to stand next to him.

"What is it?" he asked, looking into the globe.

"Oh, it's just my scryer."

"Can I touch it?"

"Of course."

Seth laid his hands on the glass. It was warm. He looked closer. "Should it be doing that?" he said.

There was a small storm gathering in the centre of the globe, a whirlpool of purple and blue clouds flashing tiny bolts of lightning.

"No, it shouldn't," Skarla said. She turned and looked at him in wonder. "No, it shouldn't. . ."

But Seth was staring at the storm, watching as it grew. He leaned closer as it swelled to fill the sphere.

There were shapes in the clouds.

2

He is in a house, but the house is evil. The evil is everywhere and all around. He is walking up a narrow, rickety stairway but he can feel the things that swarm in the dark and lurk at the edges of this place. Hungry things, drawn here and unable to leave.

Restless like ghosts, deadly horrors.

They are protecting what lies within.

At the top of the stairs is a door. Seth pushes it open.

Beyond is an attic. It's raining hard against the skylight. Lightning flickers, and a second afterward the sky explodes with a roar.

The attic is a mess, cluttered with heaps of junk, scattered with balled-up paper. The shadows hide most of the room. There is a man at the far end. At least, it might be a man.

He is enormous. His shoulders are huge, like his arms. He is hunched over something, frantically working. He is bent so close to his work that, from behind, his head is obscured by his shoulders.

It is a drawing board. He is drawing. Scattered all around are pens and inks, brushes, artist's tools.

He is Grendel. He is the one who draws the comics. Seth knows this, like you know things in a dream.

Seth goes closer. He approaches from behind.

There is a quizzical grunt. Grendel stops drawing. He knows there is someone behind him. It's impossible, because Seth isn't even there, but Grendel knows anyway.

He raises his head. There's a little thatch of black hair on top of his head. There's something wrong with the shape of his skull.

He turns around.

3

Seth was thrown back from the globe with a cry. It was as if an invisible hand had suddenly pushed him in the chest. He fell to the earth floor of Skarla's home.

"What *are* you doing?" Justin asked, bemused.

Seth looked up at Skarla. "I saw him!" he blurted. "I saw Grendel!"

"You saw *what*?" said Kady, coming out of her chair. She hurried over as he got to his feet. "You saw Grendel? What did he look like?"

"I mean . . . I didn't really *see*, I just . . . it was him. He was this massive guy painting in an attic. I just knew it was him. I think he realized I was watching, and he didn't like it."

"Amazing," murmured Skarla, studying the globe. The clouds had gone, and it was clear again. "That thing doesn't respond to just anyone. It takes *power* to activate an artefact like that."

"I didn't do anything," Seth said.

"Then I rather suspect something has been done to *you*. You passed through the shrine, didn't you?"

"The huntress on the pedestal: who is she?" Seth asked.

"She is the Lack. One of the Six, that once ruled this realm until Tall Jake usurped it."

"I took her bow. I used it to destroy the Mort-Beast."

"Then perhaps you have earned her favour," said Skarla. "Be careful, then. The Lack's friendship can be as dangerous as her displeasure."

"What did she do to Seth?" Kady demanded.

"Now *that*," said Skarla, "is a big question."

"We need to know what happened!" Kady said.

"No," said Justin. He got up from his chair with

353

an air of resignation, and walked over to them.

"No?" said Seth.

"Ask her about Tall Jake. Ask her how to stop him. That's more important."

"Ask her about what the Lack did to you!" Kady said.

"It's two against one, honey," Justin said.

"Don't call me *honey*!" she snapped. She turned back to Seth. "That woman did something. Something inside you. Don't you want to know what?"

"Of course I do," said Seth. "But we only get one question. Tall Jake is the cause of all of this. We have to deal with him."

Kady snorted and folded her arms. "Fine. Do whatever."

Seth looked at Justin. "You sure?"

"Mate, I'm gonna find Havoc. One way or another," he said. "But I got time. Maybe I'll take a bit of a nose around Malice, ask about a little." He motioned to Skarla. "Who knows when we're gonna get a chance to talk to someone like this again. You need answers more than I do. Ask her about Tall Jake."

Seth drew a breath to say something, some words that would be enough to express his gratitude, but Justin held his hand up.

"Don't make a big deal out of it," he warned.

Seth nodded, and simply said, "Thanks."

"Y'welcome."

Seth turned to Skarla. "How do we defeat Tall Jake?"

Skarla shuffled back to the globe and laid her many

root-fingers across its surface. "Are you sure that's your question?"

"That's our question."

"Very well," said Skarla, and closed her eyes.

She was quite still for some time. The storm gathered inside the globe, swelling until the roiling clouds pressed against the glass. Justin, Seth and Kady watched her uncertainly.

"You think she's—" Justin began, but was interrupted by a booming voice that made them all jump.

Find the Shard, it said, seeming to come from the walls all around them. The jars on the shelves in the alcove rattled. Tatyana woke up and raised her head with a quizzical growl.

Seth became aware of a noise, low and hissing and huge. Waves, crashing on rocks. Wet salt spray misted against his face. He could feel a cold wind, and his clothes and hair flapped as it pushed around him.

Tall Jake has enemies, said the voice. It was deep, with a crunching undertone, as of rocks grinding together. It was like the voice of an earthquake. **The greatest of them is the Shard. Tall Jake wears the scars of their final battle on his face**.

And now they were *seeing* it. They stood on a jagged, broken shore, and the day was dark as night beneath the black clouds churning overhead. A terrible storm pounded the sky, and thunder barrelled from horizon to horizon. Dark waves smashed and jostled, sending geysers of white spray high into the air.

There, on the horizon, was another kind of storm. Flashes of strange light, explosions. A creature, vast and sinuous, swam up into the sky: a blaze of light, a distant, dazzling squiggle. Then, from the depths, something enormous rose forth and enwrapped the light in many dark tentacles. It plunged back into the water, pulling down the long, winding strip of light with it.

The battle was long, but at last the Shard was dragged to the depths by a great sea beast, summoned by Tall Jake. Knowing he was defeated, the Shard used the last of his power to transform himself and his attacker into an ornament, a trinket, small enough to go unnoticed by his enemy. The Shard imprisoned himself in a cocoon, to wait for rebirth when the time was right.

There followed a swift burst of images, moments in time that ran through their minds and before their eyes in a flurry.

The ornament rests on the seabed, crushed by the suffocating cold of the ocean. A twinkle of light comes from deep within.

An enormous fish swoops down, attracted by the light, and swallows it.

The fish is pulled on to a boat by strange fisher-folk, who seem half-fish themselves.

The fish, hanging from a hook on the dockside, is cut open with a knife. In the tumble of guts, the ornament falls out.

A bustling market, though few there are human. A

stall. The ornament sits among other ornaments. Bartering. Agreement. Payment.

And the ornament is gone.

The vision ended abruptly, and they were back in Skarla's room, in the firelight and the warmth, surrounded by the good smell of dry earth. Kady looked at Seth in alarm. She knew what he knew.

The Shard yet lives. Find the Shard. Once you have him, the remainder of the Six may join you, if you can find them and persuade them to your cause. Alone, they were defeated. Together, they can destroy Tall Jake.

The rumbling in the earth faded, and Skarla's shoulders slumped. She took her hands from the globe and sighed wearily. She ambled over to the pool and settled herself into it again, facing them.

"You have your answer," she said. "And it is not an easy road. The enemy of your enemy is your friend, but the Six are unpredictable and dangerous, and no doubt they are hidden well. If Tall Jake finds them, he will destroy them once and for all."

Kady put her hand on Seth's arm. She'd gone pale. "Um. I don't think they're hidden well enough."

"How so?" Justin asked.

"We know where the Shard is," she said. "He's sitting on the bookshelf in my bedroom."

Three Are Divided

1

"We have to go back!"

"Hey, wait," Justin protested. "Will someone clue me in here? You've got Tall Jake's most powerful enemy resting on your *bookshelf*?"

"That ornament, that one we saw just now?" Kady said. "I have it at home. I brought it back with me from Malice. I just didn't know what it *was*. I didn't remember anything after I returned. I don't even know how I *got* it!" She pulled off her beanie in frustration and scrunched it in her hands. "God, I almost brought it with me and that stupid moggy stopped me."

Justin opened his mouth to make a smart comment, then wisely shut it again at a glare from Kady.

"Let's put this together," said Seth. "Alright, since Marlowe turned up soon after you moved to Hathern, and since he can evidently *spell*, we can be pretty sure that he was an emissary of the Queen of Cats, just like Andersen was. Right?"

Kady made a distracted noise of agreement.

"Then the Queen of Cats didn't want you to bring the Shard back to Malice with you, right?"

"Right."

"So why would that be?"

"Because if Tall Jake finds the ornament, the Shard will be lost, and so will all hope of defeating him," Skarla creaked. Seth looked at her, surprised. "I have no love for Tall Jake. This land has gone to ruin since he threw down the Six and became ruler."

"They couldn't risk that I'd get caught with the Shard," Kady said. She thought for a moment. "That must mean Tall Jake doesn't know I have it. They must have figured that the safest thing was to leave it where it was and let me lead Scratch away from it." Her eyes widened. "It's in my house! Mom and Dad!"

"Whoa!" said Seth. "Don't panic. If Tall Jake doesn't know you have the Shard, then your folks are safe as long as you're gone."

"But what if he finds out?" Kady said, pacing in agitation. "Why was Scratch even chasing me in the first place, if not for the Shard? He said he remembered me from the comic, and that they'd been after me for a long while. I must have done something *else*. What did I do when I was here?" She spun around. "Seth, I have to get back. I have to get that thing out of my house!"

"You *can't* go back. If you go back home, you'll forget everything that happened here."

Realization lit up Kady's face.

"I can't," she said. "But *you* can."

2

"You want to *hypnotize* me?" Seth asked.

"Right. Listen, when someone like Henry Galesworth comes back from Malice, their memories are suppressed. But they're not *gone*. I got Henry remembering, didn't I?"

"Yeah, right before he completely flipped out."

"That's just detail," said Kady dismissively, waving a hand. "What I'm saying is, those memories are still there to access. So if you go in there prepared, you can get them back."

"Prepared how?" Justin asked.

"I give him a post-hypnotic command. A deep subconscious message that will tell him to remember everything that happened here when he encounters the trigger. The trigger can be anything: a sight, a smell, a sound, whatever. But when he finds it, it'll pull back all those memories that have been suppressed." She nibbled her bottom lip and looked at Seth uncertainly. "At least, that's the theory."

"You sure?" said Seth, doubt in his tone. "Last time you tried to hypnotize me I fell asleep."

"Well I'll do it *better* this time!" she snapped, exasperated by his lack of enthusiasm. "Or does anyone *else* have a plan?"

"Can't you just write it down or something? Pin it to his chest and shove him through?" Justin suggested.

"Do you have anything to write with?"

"Don't *you*? You brought everything including the

kitchen sink and most of the neighbour's plumbing in that rucksack. You didn't bring a pen and paper?"

"I'd just been told to run for my life by a *cat*! Gathering stationery wasn't the uppermost thing in my mind, y'know?"

"It wouldn't work, anyway," said Seth. "You saw how Henry reacted at the sight of a copy of Malice. If you gave me a note I might just throw it away or chuck a fit or something. It's too risky."

"So you'll do it?"

"Kady. . ." he said with a sigh.

"You have to, Seth! I can't hypnotize myself, and I'm not sending *him*." She made a vague gesture towards Justin.

"Cheers very much," he said sarcastically. "I wouldn't go anyway. I got my own stuff to take care of."

She ignored him, appealing to Seth. "Apart from anything else, my parents don't know him and they'd never let him take the ornament. You're the only one who can do it. You have to get that thing out of my house before Tall Jake realizes where it is. It's my mom and dad, Seth. If they get in his way. . ." She trailed off, then suddenly grabbed him by the shoulders. "*Please!*"

Justin rubbed his hand over his short black hair, an uncertain look on his face. "Mate, are you sure you wanna do this? You really wanna go back?"

Seth didn't answer for a while. He was thinking of the Conductor, the Chitters and the Timekeeper, of the gnawls and the Mort-Beast and being touched by the Lack. He was thinking of the world he'd glimpsed for a few moments while travelling between the Clock Tower and the Oubliette. He was thinking how he was standing in the home of an old woman who appeared to be a plant. It didn't seem particularly unusual any more.

Malice was terrifying and wonderful. Some would look at it and call it a nightmare, but Seth saw a frontier, the only New World he could ever hope to have. The Earth had been explored, mapped, tamed. The chances of getting off the planet within his lifetime were virtually zero. He lived in a dead time, and he hated it.

But here was adventure. Here was danger. Here he'd faced down monsters and defeated them. You could make a billion pounds, you could be a rock star adored by everyone, you could be the leader of a country, and the feeling still wouldn't come close.

I have need of a champion. I choose you.

After this, could he really go back to shopping at Tesco with his mum?

He was the only one who could do it, and someone had to. Because if Skarla was right, it was their only hope of stopping Tall Jake. He had to get to the Shard before Tall Jake realized where it was. He had to get it away from Kady's house. Her parents were in terrible danger until he did.

Even if meant running the risk of losing all this. Even if it meant abandoning Kady a second time.

He had no choice. It was just the way he was.

3

"Imagine you're at the top of a flight of stairs. You're going to take a walk down those steps to the landing at the bottom. There are ten steps. With each step, you will feel more relaxed."

Seth nodded drowsily. He was sitting in one of the battered chairs. The warmth of the fire and Kady's slow, measured voice had already relaxed him to the point where he could barely keep his head up.

"Now slowly walk down the stairs. One ... two ... three..."

4

The next thing Seth knew, his eyes were blinking open. He felt great. The weariness and fear of the previous days had fallen from him, and he was suddenly in a very optimistic mood.

"Did it work?" he asked Kady, who was sitting opposite him in the other chair. Tatyana had her eyes closed and was lying full-length in front of the fire. She was now functioning as a sabretoothed radiator, her metal skin having heated to scalding temperatures.

"Well, you stayed awake this time, at least," Kady said. "I guess we won't know until you get back. I've placed the post-hypnotic command in your mind. When you cross over, you'll forget just like I did, like Henry Galesworth and everyone else. But when you find the trigger, it'll all come back to you."

"What's the trigger?" he said, getting up and stretching.

"Don't worry about it, you'll only forget after I tell you," said Kady, getting up with him. "It had to be something, well, *striking*. You'll know when you see it." She gave him a weak smile. "I gave you the licence-plate number of Scratch's car as well. Remembered it from when he nearly ran me down. It'll give you something to start with, if you want to start looking for the bad guys over there."

"I'm just going to get the Shard," he said. "Then I'm coming straight back. I'll find you. I'll get back somehow and I'll find you guys. I won't forget. I promise."

Kady shook her head, eyes filling with tears. "Don't say that. I know you and promises. You'd move earth and sky to make it happen. Don't make a promise you can't keep."

He gazed at her steadily. "I'll find you. I promise."

She looked away from him, her face sad.

"Don't worry, eh?" said Justin, slapping him on the shoulder. He motioned at Tatyana. "Me and WeightWatchers over there will keep her safe for you."

Tatyana gave a low warning growl, indicating that she wasn't quite as asleep as she appeared.

Kady rolled her eyes and laughed, though half of it was a sob. "Great," she said sarcastically. "Stuck with these two jokers in a place like this." She poked Seth in the chest. "You *better* come back, and soon."

Seth turned to Skarla. "How will they get out of the Oubliette?" he asked.

"I have my own ways to the surface," she replied. "Much

quicker and safer than the way down. I will see them out."

"And what about me?"

Skarla motioned to the round wooden door. "Through there."

"That's all?"

"That's all."

Seth looked from Kady to Justin and back again. At last they'd arrived at the moment, and there was little more to say. Seth didn't dare think further about what he had to do. The most terrible thing that could happen was to forget this, to forget his new friends and Kady, to return to a world where the Dead far outnumbered the Living, with no memory of Malice. It would be like cutting out all his hopes, all his dreams, everything that was precious to him, and leaving a grey shell of a boy, like Henry Galesworth was.

He couldn't forget. He *wouldn't*.

Justin held out his hand. "Been a pleasure and a privilege," he said.

Seth clasped it and shook it. "Likewise."

Kady hugged him briefly, then pulled away, wiping her nose with the back of her hand, sniffling.

"See you later, Tatyana," Seth said. The sabretooth raised her head, blinked lazily, and then laid it down again and closed her eyes.

"Cats," said Seth. "They're all the same."

Kady burst out laughing, then threw herself at him and hugged him hard. He felt her tears touch his neck, and something ached in his stomach. He wanted to stay, he wanted to stay here so *badly*. He wanted to stay here with her.

Then she broke the hug, turned away and walked out of the room, crying.

Seth stared, shocked and slightly hurt. Justin gave him a sympathetic look.

"Mate, seriously. I'll look after her. We're gonna go find Havoc. We'll leave word where we can. You just make sure you come back."

"I'm coming back," Seth replied. "Count on it."

"One more thing," said Justin.

"What?"

"Can I get my hoodie off you?"

Seth looked down at himself. He was still wearing Justin's hoodie, which he'd put on when he was recovering from the Lack's freezing touch.

"Y'know, I wouldn't ask, but you're going home and I don't think I'm gonna be passing a TK Maxx anytime soon." Justin grinned.

Seth took it off and handed it back to him. Then, because it somehow felt the right thing to do, he hugged Justin too.

"Safe journey, mate," Justin said.

Seth nodded. He walked over to the door and pulled it open. Beyond was an earthen tunnel, thick with roots and vines that obscured whatever lay beyond. A cool breeze blew, and he knew it was the air of home, subtly different to that of Malice.

He hesitated for the barest of moments, then plunged into the tunnel, pulling the door closed behind him.

366

October

1

"And now let's ask the studio audience what they think! What's it to be? Should she gamble on the chance of a new Ford Fiesta, or take her nine hundred pounds and go home?"

The camera panned across the audience, dozens of faces, all yelling advice. Most of the advice was to gamble. The TV cut back to a nervous-looking woman with stringy brown hair who looked ten years older than she was. Standing with his arm around her shoulders was a well-groomed presenter with teeth bright enough to stun an ox.

"I don't know, Tim. It's nine hundred pounds. . ."

"Oh, just take the money, you dizzy crone!" Seth's dad snapped at the screen. "You'd only crash that car if you had it!"

Seth's eyes flicked wearily to his dad, then back to the TV. He was sprawled on the sofa with his cheek resting on one fist, bored enough to die where he lay.

Dad's in Dad's Chair, Mum's in Mum's Chair, and all's right with the world, he thought scornfully. Except all *wasn't* right with the world. Because his friend Luke and his friend Kady were gone, and he had no idea what had happened to them or where they were.

Maybe, just maybe, they'd be coming back one day. They'd pop up out of nowhere, like he did. They'd be found wandering in the woods out near Hathern, covered in leaves and roots, dirty and half-starved. Until that time, he was alone here. His friends were gone, and all that was left was this.

The other kids in the village didn't trust him, and some of the parents openly hated him. At first there was excitement at his return. He'd been gone four days, Kady for half that time, Luke for much longer. But soon they realized that he hadn't brought them answers. He didn't know where his friends were. He didn't know what had happened. He just didn't remember.

Either that, or he was lying. Some of them thought that. A *lot* of them thought that. It was much more likely than amnesia.

He *knew* where Kady and Luke were, they said. Why? Because he *killed* them! And he'd faked his own disappearance to throw them off the trail.

The police took his clothes away for examination and came back with strange stories of foreign elements in the dirt, things they couldn't identify. That, and some strands of Kady's hair.

They'd told his parents he shouldn't leave Hathern for a while. They might need to question him further. They might need to press charges.

Psychologists came and talked to Seth, but they couldn't get through. When it got into the papers, Mrs Galesworth got in touch with the police and told them that she recognized the boy who traumatized her son. Eyebrows were raised. Such similar cases. DNA evidence was compared, and it was confirmed that the dirt on Seth was from the same place as specks they'd tested from Henry when he first returned. They'd both been there and both come back with their memories blanked.

Reporters weighed in. Seth told them he didn't know anything. He had a vague feeling that having his face in the papers was a Bad Thing, that drawing attention to himself was Not Very Clever, but he didn't understand why. Besides, he was miserable and couldn't care less.

Articles got printed. At first in paranoid conspiracy rags, and later in the nationals. Dad moaned about the disruption in their lives and Mum used it as an excuse to get her hair cut.

They made it on to the news. Mum gushed on camera about how lucky they were to have their boy back and how desperately they'd missed him. Dad sat silently next to her, looking supportive.

Seth hardly noticed it all. He was restless. He knew he was supposed to be doing something. He just couldn't remember what.

The woman on the game show decided to keep the money in the face of the crowd's derisive jeering. "First sensible thing she's done," Dad commented. Mum looked disappointed. She'd been hoping for the heady thrill of a gamble.

Oh well. There was always tomorrow's show.

2

Three weeks passed, and Seth's story waned. There was no new evidence, and not enough to prosecute him. Forensic pathologists couldn't make head or tail of the foreign matter on his clothes, and Kady's hair could have been stuck on him for days. It didn't prove he'd been with her after she disappeared.

It was a mystery, but mysteries need fuel to feed them, and there was no more to be had. Then one of the big daily papers uncovered a story about a government minister and his secret mistress, and everyone had something new to be scandalized about. The reporters stopped hanging about the village. The phone stopped ringing.

"Ah, peace and quiet," said Seth's dad, although his routine of work-TV-sleep had scarcely changed even when the furore was at its peak. Mum made noises of agreement and quietly lamented the passing of her fifteen minutes of fame. She stopped wearing nice clothes and went back to shapeless things from discount stores.

The new term had already started, so Seth went back to school. Everyone treated him like he was a bomb.

Kady and Luke didn't come home.

3

It was a blustery day in early October, and he was walking back down the lane from where his bus dropped him off when someone called his name.

He'd been trailing the other kids, as usual. He didn't like walking with them. He felt different from them now, and they sensed that and ignored him.

He stopped and turned around. Standing in the sheltered

driveway of a nearby house was a man. He'd clearly been waiting there for Seth to pass.

"What's up?" Seth asked, a little warily. At first, he'd suspected a reporter, but one look at this guy told him otherwise. He was one of the freaks who thought Seth had been abducted by aliens. There'd been a few, and they all looked strange.

The man stepped closer. He was easily a foot taller than Seth, wearing a waistcoat over a white shirt and grey trousers held up by braces. As he approached, he took off his fedora and mopped his brow with a handkerchief. There was no hair on his head, or on his face, even on his eyebrows. He looked like he was made of dough.

"Seth Harper," he said, his voice high and girlish, with a soft lisp.

Definitely one of the alien crackpots, Seth thought. "What do you want?" he asked.

"You don't remember me?"

"Should I?"

The man bent closer, his piggy, dark eyes narrowed. *What is this guy's problem?* Seth thought, leaning back to get away from his milky breath.

"Look closely."

"Listen, you nutbag, I don't know who you are, and I don't care!" Seth snapped, pushing him back by the shoulders. He had a short temper nowadays, and a habit of picking fights. "Get out of my face!"

The man straightened and studied him for a short while.

"What?" Seth demanded. "Go chase some flying saucers or something."

"You really don't know me," the man said slowly. Then he gave Seth a quick smile and popped his hat back on his head. "How very fortunate for you."

He walked off up the lane back towards the main road. Seth watched him go.

"Wow," he said. "*That* was weird."

Then he realized that was something Kady would have said, and he spent the rest of the day depressed.

4

Two days later, Seth found himself experiencing the uncomfortable sensation of being followed.

The weather had gone suddenly bitter, an early taste of the winter to come. Seth was walking around the village because it was something to do, and because he couldn't bear being inside all day.

He had no friends in Hathern any more. They'd united against him for fear of being cast out themselves. So he went walking a lot, just to kill time.

He was heading down the road by the church when he began to feel he was being watched. He scanned the road, but saw nobody. It was a Sunday afternoon, and the streets were empty. The kids were hanging about down the reccy ground and the adults were on their post-Sunday-lunch comedown, slumped in front of their TVs.

The feeling persisted all around Hathern until he'd made a complete circuit and was almost back home. That was when he caught sight of Marlowe, Kady's silver tabby, padding along the drystone wall of the graveyard. The cat hopped down and started trotting along behind Seth.

"Was it you?" he asked, crouching down and offering his hand. Marlowe graciously accepted a vigorous head-scrub. "You been following me about? I haven't seen you for ages."

He petted Marlowe for a bit and then got up to go. Marlowe followed behind.

"Go on, cat," he said. "Go home. I bet they miss you back there."

Marlowe paid no attention.

"Fine, do what you like," said Seth. But when he got to his doorstep, the cat was still on his heels.

"You're not coming in," he told Marlowe. "Go on, shoo!"

Marlowe blinked and stared at him. Seth picked him up and dumped him out on the pavement.

By the time he'd returned to the doorstep, the cat was there.

Seth opened the door a crack, just enough to slide in without letting the cat past, but the cat got in anyway through some kind of unholy contortion and ended up sitting in the hallway while Seth swore at him.

"Watch your language!" called Dad from the lounge, over the sound of the news. They were interviewing the government minister's wife, who was tearfully asking the world to forgive her wayward husband.

Seth picked up the cat, tossed him out of the door, and slammed it shut. The cat began to yowl. Seth ignored him. Eventually Dad stormed out of the lounge.

"What on earth is that racket?" he demanded, striding for the door.

"It's a cat, don't open the—"

But Dad wasn't listening. He threw open the door and the cat bolted in and ran up the stairs. Seth swore again and Dad clipped him round the ear.

It took a ten-minute hunt before they found the cat in a cupboard, and this time Seth picked him up and carried him out, muttering curses. The cat purred contentedly in his arms all the way back to Kady's house.

He stood in the driveway for a while. Though the house was very large, it wasn't especially grand. They were never a family that showed off their money much. It was set at the end of a cul-de-sac, and Seth hadn't been back here or even passed by since his reappearance. He knew what people said about him. He didn't want to face Kady's parents.

He put the cat down in the drive and started to walk away, but he'd only gone twenty yards when he heard a meow from behind and realized Marlowe was still following him. His head bowed.

"Alright, cat, you win," he said. He scooped up Marlowe and rang the doorbell.

It was Greg who answered. He'd always been thin, but now he looked gaunt. His hair was greyer than Seth remembered. There was a flicker of surprise on his face at the sight of Seth.

"Sorry, Mr Blake," he said. "I brought back your cat. He won't stop following me."

He held out Marlowe. Greg took him dazedly.

"He's been gone for days. We didn't think he'd be coming back," Greg said. "Thank you."

Seth shrugged. There was an awkward silence.

"Would you like to come in?" Greg said.

"Mr Blake, I want you to know that I'd never do anything to . . . I mean, even though I don't know what happened, I'd never have hurt her. Never. And I know she's okay somewhere, she's just—"

"Please don't," said Greg quickly. Then, gentler: "Let's not talk about that. I know you'd never do . . . what they said you did." He stroked the cat distractedly in his arms.

"How's Mrs Blake?"

"She's . . . she's not doing too well. She's in therapy. That's where she is now, in fact. I don't know that it's helping much." His face went suddenly desperate. "If there's *anything* you can tell me that might—"

"I swear, Mr Blake. God knows I've tried to remember, but I can't. I just *can't*."

Greg looked crestfallen. He stooped and put the cat down in the hallway.

"Would you like to go up to her room?" he said. "Maybe it might, you know . . . you might remember something."

"I don't think it'll help, Mr Blake," said Seth, who wanted

the ground to swallow him up. To see his friend's father so broken was killing him.

"Please," said Greg, barely more than a whisper. "Try."

Seth couldn't refuse a plea like that. "Okay," he said. "Sure, no problem."

The cat ran up the stairs ahead of him and into Kady's room. He frowned at him as he went, and tried to ignore the absurd suspicion that he had been trying to *lead* him here. Greg didn't follow them but retreated into the kitchen, perhaps hoping that Seth might have some revelation if given enough time on his own.

Seth pushed open the door and stepped into the bedroom. Everything was as it had been. A bit tidier than usual, perhaps, but the same: bed, computer, wardrobe. Without Kady in it, it was just a room.

Marlowe meowed, and he turned to find the cat sitting on top of the bookcase.

"You," he said, "are one great big pain in the—"

But then he stopped, as his gaze fell on what *else* was on the bookshelf. It was an ornament. Kady's strange ornament that she'd brought back from San Francisco.

Or *was* it San Francisco? Suddenly he wasn't sure. But where *else* could it have been from?

He walked over to the bookcase, fascinated, *drawn*. He picked the ornament up and studied it closely. What an ugly beast it was: a grey stone monster, its tentacles enclosing an egg made of some kind of white, semi-opaque mineral.

Something was nagging at him. A voice in the back of his mind, which had been whispering for weeks now, had suddenly risen in volume.

I've placed a post-hypnotic command in your mind.

When you find the trigger, it'll all come back to you.

Where did he know those lines from? Had he heard them in a movie or something? And why did he have a string of numbers and letters running round in his head? A licence plate? Why was he thinking of a licence plate?

I'll find you. I promise.

He had said that! He remembered saying it! But when? When?

Marlowe was watching Seth carefully from his vantage point on top of the bookshelf, but Seth couldn't take his eyes off the ornament in his hand. He was staring at the egg. It turned the light in a curious way. Almost as if there was something small inside, a little worm of brightness, like the filament in a bulb, that writhed and twisted fitfully.

As Seth held the ornament in his hands, the egg began to glow. First dimly, then bright as flame, illuminating his astonished face from beneath.

"I'll find you," he whispered. "I promise."

STILL HERE, DEAR READER? STILL ENJOYING YOUR LITTLE TOUR OF MY DOMAIN? I'M SO VERY GLAD. AFTER ALL, MALICE WOULD BE NOTHING WITHOUT YOU.
SETH HAS ESCAPED ME, IT SEEMS. BUT I STILL HAVE HIS FRIENDS. WOULD YOU HAVE FARED BETTER IN HIS PLACE? ARE YOU BRAVE ENOUGH TO FIND OUT? PERHAPS YOU WILL BE THE STAR OF THE NEXT ISSUE.
YOU ONLY HAVE TO ASK.
I'LL BE BACK SOON, DEAR READER. AND SO WILL YOU.

The story continues in

Coming soon

www.malicecomic.co.uk